WEAPONS OF THE
CIVIL WAR CAVALRYMAN

JOHN WALTER
Series Editor Martin Pegler

Illustrated by Adam Hook & Alan Gilliland

OSPREY PUBLISHING
Bloomsbury Publishing Plc
Kemp House, Chawley Park, Cumnor Hill, Oxford OX2 9PH, UK
1385 Broadway, 5th Floor, New York, NY 10018, USA
E-mail: info@ospreypublishing.com
www.ospreypublishing.com

OSPREY is a trademark of Osprey Publishing Ltd

First published in Great Britain in 2020

A catalog record for this book is available from the British
Library.

ISBN: PB 9781472842237; eBook 9781472842244;
ePDF 9781472842213; XML 9781472842220

20 21 22 23 24   10 9 8 7 6 5 4 3 2 1

Index by Rob Munro
Typeset by PDQ Digital Media Solutions, Bungay, UK
Printed and bound in India by Replika Press Private Ltd.

Osprey Publishing supports the Woodland Trust, the UK's
leading woodland conservation charity.

To find out more about our authors and books visit
www.ospreypublishing.com. Here you will find extracts, author
interviews, details of forthcoming events and the option to sign
up for our newsletter.

Dedication
To Alison, Adam, Nicky, Findlay, Georgia and Holly – yet again!

Acknowledgments
I would like to thank Sarah Stoltzfus of Morphy Auctions for
providing many of the excellent images, and Tim Prince of
College Hill Arsenal not only for illustrations but also for access
to his exceptional knowledge of Civil War weapons. Matt Parise
of Rock Island Auctions also helped to improve the picture
content, and the US Patent and Trademark Office website was an
invaluable resource. Nick Reynolds of Osprey helped to shape
the project, Paul Scarlata and Martin Pegler continue to be
supportive, and I am very grateful for the assistance offered by
members of the Osprey author community for filling gaps in my
knowledge by identifying the uniforms and accoutrements
featured in the color plates.

Artist's note
Readers may care to note that the original paintings from which
the color plates in this book were prepared are available for
private sale. All reproduction copyright whatsoever is retained by
the publishers. All inquiries should be addressed to:

scorpiopaintings@btinternet.com

The publishers regret that they can enter into no correspondence
upon this matter.

Front cover, above: An M1860 .56-56 Spencer Carbine,
no. 37201. These guns proved to be among the most effective
weapons in the cavalryman's armory, serving throughout the
Civil War. Spencers were also made by the Burnside Rifle
Company of Providence, Rhode Island, which had delivered
30,496 of a 35,000-gun order by the end of 1865. By June 30,
1866, Spencer and Burnside had delivered 12,471 rifles and
94,196 carbines into Federal stores, though only about 50,000
carbines had been issued when hostilities ceased. (Morphy
Auctions, www.morphyauctions.com)

Front cover, below: Major General Philip Henry Sheridan and
"The Fight with Stuart's Cavalry at Yellow Tavern," a lithograph
by Edwin Austin Forbes (1839–95). (National Archives,
Washington, DC)

Title-page illustration: Printed in France, this illegibly signed
print shows a sergeant of the 6th Pennsylvania Cavalry (Rush's
Lancers) in action in 1862. Note that he carries a lance and an
M1840 or M1860 cavalry saber. Lances were made only in small
numbers, and then only at the beginning of the war for issue to a
mere handful of cavalrymen, such as the 6th Pennsylvania
Cavalry. (Anne S.K. Brown Military Collection, https://library.
brown.edu/collections)

CONTENTS

INTRODUCTION   4

DEVELOPMENT   8
The march of technology

USE   48
Weapons and war

IMPACT   71
Weapons: fact and fiction

CONCLUSION   75

APPENDIX: US PATENTS   77

SELECT BIBLIOGRAPHY   79

INDEX   80

INTRODUCTION

A First Model .44-caliber Colt six-shot Dragoon revolver, no. 4767. The first Dragoons (1848–50) had a square-back trigger guard and ovoid cylinder-stop slots. The Second Model (1850–51) had squared cylinder-stop slots, pins between the nipples, a roller on the hammer, and a leaf-type main spring, while the perfected or Third Model (1851–61) not only had a round-back trigger guard and an improved back sight but could also accept a shoulder stock. The Dragoon revolvers were Colt's first major success; about 20,000 were made in 1849–55, 9,380 of which were purchased by the US Army. (Morphy Auctions, www.morphyauctions.com)

While cavalry units served in the Continental Army (1776–83) and in the US Army from 1792 until the end of the War of 1812 in March 1815, for part of its early history the army of the United States lacked a mounted element. In June 1832, however, increasingly mindful of territorial expansion and the need to patrol frontiers, Congress approved an experimental Battalion of Mounted Rangers. The value of these horsemen soon became obvious, and the Regiment of US Dragoons – armed with Hall carbines – was duly authorized on March 2, 1833. The 2d Dragoons, also armed with Hall carbines, was raised in 1836 and a Regiment of Mounted Riflemen equipped with the M1841 "Mississippi" caplock rifle followed in May 1846.

On May 9, 1846, the charge of a squadron of the 2d Dragoons, led by Captain Charles Augustus May, played an important role in the dispersal of Mexican artillerymen during the battle of Resaca de la Palma, the second engagement of the Mexican–American War (1846–48). The future of horsemen in the US Army was assured. War with Mexico also showed the value of the Walker Colt revolver, despite severe teething troubles, and the Colt Dragoon revolver was adopted in 1848. When the first two US cavalry regiments were raised in 1855, therefore, they were given .36-caliber Colt Navy revolvers to supplement their sabers. Statistically among the most important Federal purchases during the Civil War, the .36 Colt Navy revolver or "Old Model Belt Pistol" (Model of 1851) would be manufactured in large numbers: 215,348 at Colt's factory in Hartford, Connecticut, alone. Its naval connotation arose from the maritime scene rolled into the cylinder periphery, honoring the victory of the Texans over the Mexicans on May 16, 1843 at the naval battle of Campeche. In 1855, 1,000 Colt Navy revolvers were purchased by the US Army, with square-back trigger guards and a barrel wedge above the retaining screw. Minor changes were subsequently made, and shoulder stocks – never popular – were offered after 1859.

Leakage of gas at the breech became significantly worse as the Hall carbines aged, so, on March 12, 1847, to enable the "remounting" of the 2d Dragoons proposed in 1844, a .69-caliber smoothbore musketoon was introduced for artillery, cavalry, and sappers. The three versions differed in minor respects: cavalry issue, for example, lacked bayonets. When assembly ceased in 1859, 6,703 M1847 cavalry musketoons had been made in Springfield Armory. Many survivors were converted after the introduction of the Springfield-made .58-caliber M1855 "rifle carbine" and pistol carbine to fire Minié expanding cylindro-conoidal bullet ammunition. Production of the M1855 caplock rifle carbine amounted to a mere 1,020 in 1855–56, in two patterns, while 4,021 M1855 pistol carbines were made in 1856–57.

Turning to edged weapons, many cavalrymen – especially officers – regarded the saber as their principal weapon, even though dragoons were often intended to fight dismounted. The only types of saber issued to cavalrymen when the Civil War fighting began in April 1861 were the M1833 dragoon, M1840 heavy, and M1860 light-cavalry patterns for rank-and-file soldiers, and, of course, better-quality versions – often with decoratively etched blades – for officers.

Escalating conflict over opposition to the expansion of slavery into newly created territories, and then the election of Republican President Abraham Lincoln on November 6, 1860, persuaded South Carolina to secede from the Union on December 20, 1860. The Union duly began to unravel. On April 12, 1861, the momentous attack on Fort Sumter, one of several Union forts located in Charleston harbor, by Confederate forces began; it proved to be the catalyst for a catastrophic four-year Civil War in which hundreds of thousands were to die. It was also to be the first conflict in which breech-loading and metal-case cartridges were used in quantity.

Although it has been suggested that the likelihood of war promoted the development of so many breech-loaders in such a short time, the catalysts were actually ever-growing industrialization – particularly in New England – and the antebellum introduction of rifle-muskets and revolvers, respectively increasing the range of engagement and rate of fire. Westward expansion, encouraging the creation not only of new states but also their militia forces, was another factor. The manufacturing base, initially dominant in Pennsylvania, gradually moved northeastward to New England where it remained when the Civil War began. There had been no shortage of invention or, indeed, technological advance. Much of this was due to the

The M1855 long-barrel pistol carbine, with the detachable butt in place. Note the Maynard tape primer ahead of the hammer. The long-barrel pistol carbines, with surprisingly sophisticated 400yd back sights, were specifically intended to replace M1847 musketoons serving the cavalrymen. Offering far better performance and greater handiness, they were popular with dragoons, who often fought dismounted, but other cavalrymen hated them: objections included the change in point-of-impact (real or perceived) when fired with the stock attached, and additional weight compared with the .54-caliber M1842 caplock pistol. (Morphy Auctions, www.morphyauctions.com)

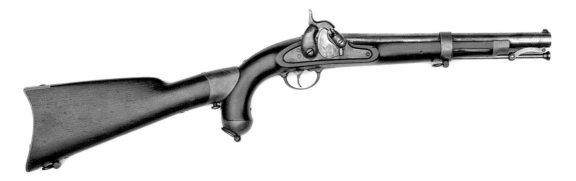

An Ames-made M1833 officer's dragoon saber, with decoratively etched blade. Based loosely on the British P1822 light-cavalry saber, the M1833 was issued to the two regiments of dragoons. It had a 34in pipe-backed blade, a brass multi-bar hilt, and a leather grip wrapped with twisted brass wire. The one-piece steel scabbard had two suspending rings and a prominent drag on the chape. (Morphy Auctions, www.morphyauctions.com)

Nicknamed "Old Wristbreaker," the heavyweight M1840 cavalry saber was not universally popular. This example was made in Hartford, Connecticut, by Collins & Company. The M1840 had a three-bar guard and a heavy blade with a single fuller on each side. It was superseded shortly before the war began by the generally similar but lighter M1860. (Morphy Auctions, www.morphyauctions.com)

concept of interchangeability: something that was alien to many gunmakers, but vital to the production and maintenance of thousands of weapons.

Initially, neither protagonist could equip their men effectually. A short-term answer lay in the retrieval of guns held in store, refurbishing them where appropriate. Conversions from flintlock to caplock were undertaken, particularly in the Confederacy, where firearms were in notably short supply and manufacturing capacity was minimal. Anything which could shoot was impressed into service, including long rifles and shotguns, while purchases of guns were to be unparalleled in military history. The burgeoning entrepreneurial capabilities of industry allowed an incredible variety of guns to be offered to both protagonists almost from the outset of hostilities. Not only did the war provide a unique chance to try out the merits of competing designs under combat conditions, but it made and also sometimes lost many a promoter's fortune.

Not everyone was convinced that the broadening of sources of supply was beneficial, however. Colonel James Wolfe Ripley, the new Chief of Ordnance, wrote on June 17, 1861 to Secretary of War Simon Cameron, noting that the introduction of arms of too many types, kinds, and chamberings was one of the worst things that could happen in military service by complicating, in particular, the manufacture and supply of ammunition. Ripley was determined to equip the US Army only with simple and serviceable firearms that accepted the ammunition that was already being made in the government arsenals. Nothing else should be accepted, he stated, and the weapons procured by individual states under the terms of the Militia Act of 1808 should be obtained only through Ordnance Department channels. Nothing revolutionary or departing from standard, therefore, should ever be issued (Lewis 1956: 159).

In the North, manufacturing capacity, considerable though it was, could not cope with demand. Consequently, much military equipment, including firearms and edged weapons, had to be imported from Europe. According to the *Statement of ordnance and ordnance stores purchased by the Ordnance Department from January 1, 1861, to June 30, 1866*, Federal purchases included 372,823 revolvers, 396,896 breech-loading carbines, 428,292 Enfield rifle-muskets, 1,472,614 Springfield rifle-

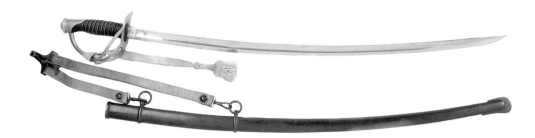

THE BLOCKADE ON THE "CONNECTICUT PLAN".

The US Mail side-paddle-wheel steamer USMS *Nashville*, captured in Charlestown harbor when the Civil War began on April 12, 1861 and pressed into Confederate naval service, leaves the "old tubs" of the blockaders in her wake in this Currier & Ives print of 1862. "Running Ships" (also known as "blockade runners" or simply "runners") transported cargos across the Atlantic to Nassau in the Bahamas, St. George's Harbour in Bermuda, Halifax in Nova Scotia, and Tampico in Mexico before making comparatively short-range dashes to Galveston, Charleston, or Wilmington. More than 60 of them used the port of Wilmington regularly, and, though about 40 had been sunk or captured by the end of the war, almost all had made more than one successful run. The ideal blockade runner was long and slender, able to pass at low tide over the bars and sandbanks that guarded so many Southern harbors. Cabins were removed to make space for guns or cotton; masts were reduced to poles; hulls were painted in neutral colors; telescoping funnels could reduce a silhouette; and feathering paddle wheels minimized white-water disturbance. Most had been designed for coastal or estuary trade, however, and were vulnerable to even a single cannon-shot. Many were lost while crossing the Atlantic, along with tens of thousands of firearms and edged weapons: for example, when the British-built screw steamer SS *Georgiana* ran ashore north of Charleston harbor on March 19, 1863 to avoid confronting the screw steam gunboat USS *Wissahickon*, 10,000 Enfields plus ammunition, swords, and $90,000 in gold were lost (Gaines 2008: 120). (Author's collection)

muskets, and 208,276,829 cartridges for the carbines alone. Among items specifically for the cavalry were 4,567 lances, 203,285 M1860 regulation-pattern sabers, 1,279 officer's sabers, and 236,393 carbine slings.

As industrialization had largely bypassed the South, where there was also a crucial shortage of raw materials, only a limited quantity of weapons could be made. Like the Union, therefore, the Confederacy turned to Europe. Precisely what was acquired at national and state level is difficult to determine, though the *Summary Statement of Over-Seas Purchases*, prepared by Chief of Ordnance for the Confederacy Josiah Gorgas for Confederate States Secretary of War James Alexander Seddon, confirms that 70,890 long and 9,715 short Enfields had been ordered by the government of the Confederacy from Britain by February 3, 1863.

When the Civil War began, the Union Navy implemented the so-called Anaconda Plan proposed by Brevet Lieutenant General Winfield "Old Fuss and Feathers" Scott: a blockade of Southern ports intended to strangle maritime trade. While the first year provided little encouragement to the Union, small Confederate craft could not hope to confront the ever-growing number of Union warships, and more and more "runners" were captured or destroyed as time passed.

Though many Britons of liberal conscience favored the North, more conservative elements were prepared to deal with the Confederacy. The South Carolina legislature was soon channeling orders for itself, and apparently also neighboring states, through John Fraser & Company of Charleston and affiliates Trenholm Brothers of New York and Fraser, Trenholm & Company of Liverpool. Nor was there a lack of entrepreneurs prepared to confront Union blockaders with ships of ostensibly British ownership: the Anglo-Confederate Shipping Company, for example, was based in Liverpool.

By the end of 1862, Britain had supplied the Federal authorities with more than 125,000 muskets and carbines, about 170,000 had come from Austria, at least 115,000 came from the German states, and large quantities of weapons had also been purchased in France and Belgium. Many were also sold to the Confederacy, meaning significant numbers saw action with mounted units on both sides.

DEVELOPMENT
The march of technology

NEW REPEATING LONGARMS IN FEDERAL HANDS

The Union Army's commander-in-chief, Brevet Lieutenant General Winfield Scott, and the Chief of Ordnance, Brevet Brigadier General Ripley, were old-school traditionalists who saw the rifle-musket and the carbine as the weapons of the infantryman and cavalryman respectively – provided that they were single-shot muzzle-loaders and did not require proprietary ammunition. Yet, statistically, the most important cavalry weapons would be breech-loading carbines and revolvers, need ensuring that virtually any design reaching production could be bought by the governments of the Union and the Confederacy; by legislatures of individual states to whom the Militia Act of 1808 had devolved responsibility for raising and equipping militia units; and even by benefactors rich enough to equip individual units.

Spencer rifles and carbines

The most influential of all the breech-loaders was the .52-bore Spencer, patented in March 1860 by the gunsmith Christopher Miner Spencer (1833–1922), who, with the assistance of fellow gunsmith Luke Wheelock (1828–1907), had produced about 30 prototypes while working for Cheney Brothers Silk Mills Company in Manchester, Connecticut. Patronage of the Cheneys, who were friendly with Secretary of the Navy Gideon Welles, encouraged a trial of the Spencer to be undertaken successfully in Washington Navy Yard on June 8, 1861. An inherent weakness was eventually found in the extractor, but an improvement was duly patented in July 1862.

On June 22, 1861, the Union Navy ordered 700 rifles from Spencer, intending to undertake large-scale trials; 600 of them were inspected in

AMMUNITION

When the Civil War began, the standard US Army infantry weapon was the rifle-musket firing Minié-type expanding bullets. Loading involved tearing the paper cartridge open, dropping the powder and then the bullet down the bore, followed by the cartridge paper, and then tamping them in place with the rammer.

The advent of the percussion cap had allowed the cap-and-nipple to be substituted for the pan and priming powder of the flintlock, but many of the breech-loading carbines still used combustible ammunition. One type of Sharps cartridge, for example, had a 1.3in linen case with the base nitrated to facilitate ignition; loaded with 58–60 grains of black powder and a 460-grain lead bullet, .907in long with a base diameter of .544in, it measured 2.03in overall.

In 1812, however, the French gunsmith Jean-Samuel Pauly (1766–c.1821) had been granted a French patent protecting a breech-loading rifle in which a spring-driven striker ignited priming compound in the base of a cartridge case made of thin brass sheet or card-like paper. By the time the French inventor Benjamin Houillier (1812–67) perfected the pinfire round or *cartouche à broche* devised by the French gunsmith Casimir Lefaucheux (1802–52) for his 1835-patent shotgun, therefore, there had been many innovations.

Walter Hunt (1796–1859) patented his Rocket Ball caseless cartridge in the United States in August 1848. The hollow-based projectile charged with primer propellant worked well, but was exceptionally corrosive. Hunt then sold his patent rights, and the firearms designers Horace Smith and Daniel Baird Wesson transformed the Hunt rifle into the Volcanic Repeater. Volcanics fired an improved Volitional Ball containing black powder and a conventional primer: power decreased, but efficiency improved. Businessmen led by Oliver Fisher Winchester acquired the rights, while Smith & Wesson patented the first commercially viable rimfire cartridge in April 1860. As early rimfire cartridges lacked power, however, the first service-issue metallic-cartridge firearms often retained external ignition.

Patented in March 1856 with his rifle, the inventor Ambrose Everett Burnside's uniquely conical cartridge was inserted in the front of the breech block when the action was open, flash from a percussion cap struck by a sidehammer passing through a hole bored centrally through the base of the metal cartridge case to ignite the powder charge. The original wrapped-foil cartridge, which had a straight-taper case, was replaced by an improvement patented by George Pratt Foster in April 1860. A circumferential groove inside the mouth of the Foster cartridge case contained sufficient wax not only to lubricate the bullet but also to improve the gas seal. Typically 2.35in long, with the characteristic bell-mouthed 1.83in case, these cartridges were loaded with a 370-grain lead bullet – .805in long with a base diameter of .536in – and about 50 grains of black powder.

Patented in its perfected form in January 1859, the Maynard cartridge had a .51in-diameter brass tube closed by a .780in-diameter steel disk soldered to the base to assist extraction; ignition was facilitated by a flash-hole in the base. One type of Maynard cartridge was 1.85in long, with a 1.22in case containing 50 grains of black powder and a 345-grain lead bullet.

In June 1857, physician Gilbert Smith patented a cartridge unique to his carbine with "a case of india-rubber cloth, or vulcanized india-rubber" to act as a breech-seal. With a central flash-hole in a base reinforced with a papier-mâché disk, rubber-case cartridges were typically 2in long, with a 1.5in case containing 50–51 grains of black powder and a .512in-diameter, 350-grain lead bullet which was .850in long. They worked surprisingly well, though ultimately they were supplanted by wrapped-foil and similar constructions.

A noteworthy step had been taken in October 1856, when the inventor George Woodward Morse patented a metal-case cartridge. A breech-loading carbine tested by the US Army in 1857 fired a self-contained cartridge with an internal primer, and conversion of 2,000 muskets to the Morse system was authorized in 1858. Work was far from complete, however, when Confederate forces seized the machinery from Harper's Ferry Armory on April 16, 1861.

Many proprietary cartridges appeared during the Civil War, an era in which great strides were made in metallurgy. Those that had been designed by Thomas Rodman and Colonel Silas Crispin and licensed to Thomas Poultney, made of lacquered paper wrapped around tin or brass sheet, improved the performance of breech-loaders such as the Smith appreciably. As the war ran its course, the ineffectual rimfire cartridges were enlarged to chamber in guns such as the Henry and Spencer. Low velocity still restricted range and accuracy, but the enlarged bullets proved to be effective.

Breech-loaders in general and repeaters in particular could fire at prodigious rates, especially if combat was sustained, but they became little more than sophisticated clubs when cartridges ran out. This was enough to damn metallic-cartridge breech-loaders in many people's eyes, underscoring the development of caplock adaptors for the rimfire Ballards and the Lefaucheux pinfire revolvers. This was a short-lived preoccupation, however, as effectual rimfire and then centerfire cartridges soon swept such novelties away.

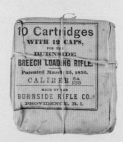

Ammunition cartons for ten .52 cartridges for the Sharps and ten .54 cartridges for the Burnside, the latter being accompanied by caps. (Rock Island Auctions, www.rockislandauction.com)

THE SPENCER EXPOSED

.56-56 M1860 Spencer Carbine

Chambered for the .56-56 Spencer rimfire round, generating 40 percent greater muzzle energy than the .44-caliber Henry rimfire, Spencer carbines had a seven-round tube magazine in the butt and a leaf-and-slider back sight. The Spencer relied on a radially moving breech block actuated by a trigger-guard lever. Opening the lever lowered the upper portion so that the two-piece block could open, allowing the extractor to pull the spent case out of the chamber and forcing the ejector to throw it out of the gun. As the trigger-guard lever closed, the tip of the breech block picked up the rim of the first cartridge in the butt-tube magazine and fed it into the chamber before the upper part of the block rose into its locked position. The M1865 Spencer carbine was fitted with the cut-off patented by the inventor Edward Stabler (1794–1883) of Sandy Springs, Maryland, which held the magazine in reserve by limiting rotation of the breech block. Few cut-off-equipped guns reached combat, however.

1. Front sight
2. Barrel
3. Rear sight
4. Seven-round magazine
5. Magazine follower
6. Magazine spring
7. Butt
8. Butt plate
9. Magazine tube base
10. Sling swivel

11. Fore stock
12. Barrel band
13. Rifled barrel
14. Breech frame
15. Cartridge in chamber
16. Cartridge extractor lever
17. Breech spring
18. Firing pin
19. Breech rod
20. Tongue

21. Tongue spring
22. Hammer (cocked)
23. Cartridges in tube magazine
24. Trigger
25. Operating lever/trigger guard
26. Breech block
27. Locking piece

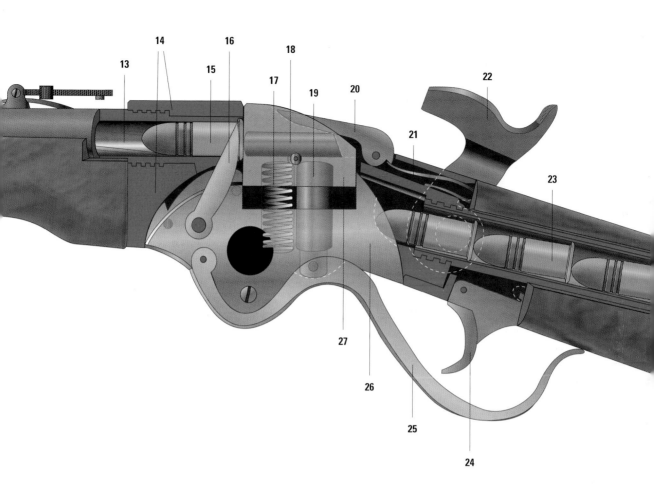

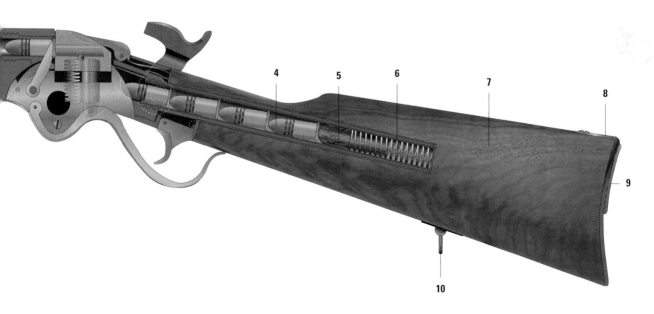

Data have been taken principally from *Instructions for Making Quarterly Returns of Ordnance and Ordnance Stores* (Washington, DC, 1865) and *Statement of ordnance and ordnance stores purchased by the Ordnance Department from January 1, 1861, to June 30, 1866* (Washington, DC, 1866).

Carbine	Caliber			Length (inches)		Weight (pounds)	Action (shots)	Guns		Cartridges	
	Nominal	Bore	Chamber	Overall	Barrel			Quantity	Price	Quantity (millions)	Price per 1,000
Ballard, 1864	.42	.42	.44	39.2	22.0	7.6	tipping block (1)	1,509	$23.29	3.53	$0.16
Burnside, 1863	.54	.54	.56	39.5	21.0	7.2	tipping block (1)	55,567	$25.42	21.82	$0.25
Cosmopolitan	.52	.50	.625	39.1	20.0	6.5	tipping block (1)	9,342	$21.39	6.30	$0.21
Gallager	.52	.51	.56	39.2	22.3	7.5	tipping barrel (1)	17,738	$22.37	8.29	$0.26
Gibbs	.52	.52	.58	39.0	22.0	7.4	tipping barrel (1)	1,052	$26.61	NA	NA
Henry	.44	.44	.46	43.5	24.0	9.3	toggle lock (15)	1,731	$36.95	4.61	$0.23
Joslyn, 1863	.52	.54	.56	38.8	22.0	6.6	side-hinged block (1)	11,261	$25.09	0.52	$0.25
Lindner	.58	.57	.60	38.8	20.0	6.1	tipping bolt (1)	892	$22.30	0.10	$0.23
Maynard, 1863	.50	.50	.55	36.9	20.0	6.0	tipping barrel (1)	20,002	$24.47	2.16	$0.33
Merrill	.54	.54	.56	37.4	22.1	6.5	sliding bolt (1)	14,495	$25.86	5.50	$0.19
Remington, 1864	.50	.52	.56	33.5	20.0	7.3	radial block (1)	20,000	$23.00	4.26	$0.16
Sharps, 1863	.52	.52	.59	38.8	22.0	8.0	dropping block (1)	80,512	$27.49	16.31	$0.21
Smith, 1864	.50	.50	.57	39.5	22.0	7.4	tipping barrel (1)	30,062	$24.80	13.86	$0.27
Spencer	.56	.52	.56	39.0	22.0	8.3	two-part radial block (7)	94,196	$25.41	58.24	$0.24
Starr	.54	.54	.60	37.6	21.0	7.4	two-part dropping block (1)	25,603	$22.92	6.86	$0.21
Warner	.50	.50	.52	37.2	20.0	7.7	side-hinged block (1)	4,001	$19.82	1.03	$0.27
Wesson	.44	.44	.46	39.5	24.0	6.9	tipping barrel (1)	151	$23.12	0.25	$0.14

December 1862 and 703 had been received by the Union Navy Ordnance Department by February 3, 1863. Some of the Union Navy trials were observed by Captain Alexander Brydie Dyer, later Chief of Ordnance, who reported positively to his superiors. The Spencer rifle passed tests favorably in November 1861, but Chief of Ordnance Ripley refused to accept it. Exasperated, Charles Cheney turned once more to Secretary of the Navy Welles, who took the unprecedented step of ordering 10,000 Spencer M1860 rifles for the Union Army.

In December 1861, the Spencer Rifle Manufacturing Company leased half the Chickering piano factory in Boston, Massachusetts, to cope with demand. No guns had been delivered by the end of January 1862, however, and, after a review of all existing government contracts, the original 10,000-gun order was reduced to 7,500. The first 500 were delivered into store on December 31, 1862, though some rifles and carbines had reached service in the winter of 1862 in the hands of volunteers. During the battle of Hoover's Gap, fought on June 24, 1863, men of Colonel John Thomas Wilder's "Lightning Brigade" were able to maul a far larger band of Confederates thanks to their privately acquired Spencer rifles.

The Henry rifle

The New Haven Arms Company of New Haven, Connecticut, faced collapse when the Civil War began, but salvation came in the form of a lever-action rifle developed from the ineffectual Volcanic repeater by the gunsmith Benjamin Tyler Henry (1821–98). Protected by a patent granted to Henry in October 1860 but assigned to the businessman Oliver Fisher Winchester (1810–80), the gun chambered a new .44 rimfire cartridge. About 13,500 Henry's Patent Repeating Rifles were made in New Haven in 1861–66. Locked by a toggle-joint beneath the bolt, operated by a swinging lever forming the trigger guard, the first guns had a bore diameter of .420in, the twist of the six-groove rifling progressively steepening from breech to muzzle. After 200 guns were made with iron frames, a reversion was made to brass and a catch was added beneath the wrist of the butt to retain the finger lever. Unlike the later Winchesters, Henry rifles lacked forends. A 24in barrel was regarded as standard, paired with an under-barrel tube magazine holding 15 rounds.

Series-made Henry rifles, available from the summer of 1862, were purchased by volunteers throughout the Civil War – perhaps 8,000 of them – even though the Federal Ordnance Department was antipathetic. After the Spencer rifle had been approved in 1863, however, attitudes softened to the extent that 1,731 Henry rifles and 4.5 million cartridges had been acquired by May 1865; government-purchase guns usually bear the marks of inspector Charles G. Chandler.

An early brass-frame Henry rifle, no. 428, with the four-part cleaning rod. The folding leaf-and-slider back sight was subsequently moved from the body to the barrel, though transitional examples are known. The advent of the Blakeslee Quickloader elevated the Spencer rifles and carbines to rank with the Henry, but none of the other breech-loaders of 1861–65 could compare so favorably. Though prone to extractor breakages, the Spencer was the more durable; Henry rifles often suffered damage to the fragile magazine tubes and had a delicate firing pin. The Henry's greatest assets were rate of fire and short-range accuracy; 20 unaimed shots could be fired in one minute with a surprisingly good chance of hitting a target. (Morphy Auctions, www.morphyauctions.com)

The .50-caliber Triplett & Scott repeating carbine. No deliveries of the potentially effectual .50-caliber Ball repeating carbine had been made when the fighting ceased, leaving the Triplett & Scott as the only other repeater to see combat. Patented in December 1864 by the gunsmith Louis Triplett of Columbia, Kentucky, it resembled a revolver rifle at a glance. The flat-sided breech block and barrel assembly, however, swung laterally to the left to eject a spent cartridge and then allow a new round from a tube magazine in the butt to enter the chamber. About 3,000 long-barrel Triplett & Scott rifles (sometimes classed as carbines) were made during the Civil War, but an order for 5,000 short-barrel guns, placed on January 2, 1865 to arm Kentucky militiamen guarding Federal supply lines, remained unfulfilled. (Rock Island Auctions, www.rockislandauction.com)

Other Union repeating longarms

The Colt-Root, M1855, or New Model revolving rifles and carbines, based on a patent granted to Elisha King Root, Colt's manufacturing superintendent, were made by Colt's Manufacturing Company of Hartford, Connecticut, from 1856 until the Hartford factory was destroyed by fire on February 4, 1864. The government had purchased 765 of them before the Southern states seceded, many ending up in Confederate hands when the Civil War began. The Union purchased additional rifles in 1861–65: 4,612 according to the records, probably including some carbines. Many of the Colts were used by regiments raised in individual states such as Ohio, including cavalrymen for whom the short-barrel carbines were preferable. Full-length rifles were used by units raised in Colorado, Illinois, Indiana, Iowa, Kansas, Kentucky, Michigan, Missouri, New York, Ohio, and Tennessee, however (Coates & McAulay 1996: 18). Despite several effectual performances, a Board of Officers convened in 1862 recommended that, owing to the prevalence of chain firing and injuries to firers, the use of Colts in the Union Army be discontinued.

FEDERAL SINGLE-SHOT CARBINES

The Sharps carbine

Born in New Jersey on January 2, 1810, Christian Sharps (1810–74) was apprenticed to a gunmaking business before finding employment at the Harper's Ferry Rifle Works in Virginia. There he worked under the

The .56-caliber Colt M1855 revolving carbine was used in surprisingly large numbers even though most soldiers disliked firing with the cylinder so close to the cheek – particularly on occasions where flash from one chamber ignited several others simultaneously. (Morphy Auctions, www.morphyauctions.com)

tutelage of the gunsmith John Hancock Hall (1781–1841) before moving to Cincinnati, Ohio, when work ceased at the Rifle Works in 1844.

Patented in September 1848, Sharps' breech mechanism consisted of a block which slid downward in the frame when the operating lever was depressed, the combustible cartridge being ignited by an externally mounted sidehammer striking a cap. Tested by the US Army as early as 1850, the first .52 carbines tested as potential cavalry weapons had the breech lever outside the trigger guard. An improved design, the so-called "Slant Breech Sharps," appeared in 1851 with the lever and trigger guard forged in one piece, a tape primer ahead of the hammer, and the hammer inside the back-action lock plate. The contours of the receiver were distinctly rounded.

Next came the M1853 or "Old Model" carbine, which provided the basis not only for Sharps carbines submitted to the US Army but also those made for trials in Britain. Old Model carbines had brass furniture, and Sharps' patented pellet magazine in the lock plate. A waterproofed priming disk, stored in a slender brass tube, was placed over the nipple each time the hammer was cocked. The 400 M1855 Sharps carbines purchased by the US Army were essentially similar, but Maynard tape primers replaced Sharps' pellet feeder. Though marked by the Sharps' Rifle Manufacturing Company of Hartford, Connecticut, they had been made by Robbins & Lawrence, also based in Hartford. Government property marks and inspector's initials will be found on the barrel.

US Army trials undertaken in 1854 with a Sharps carbine had shown accuracy to be poor, though bullet penetration in pinewood was greater than either the Hall or the carbine patented in 1838 by William Jenks, which the Army had rejected after disastrous troop trials. The action was sturdy and durable, but the sharpened upper edge of the breech block, intended to shear the base off the cartridge as the action closed, inevitably scattered a few grains of powder on the upper surface of the breech. Flash from the cap ignited the loose powder when the carbine was fired, making a worn Sharps carbine unpleasant to use: the blast could be strong enough to cut through a neckerchief tied around the breech.

The first gas-check to be used successfully was an expanding collar patented in April 1856 by the inventor and manufacturer Hezekiah Conant (1827–1902). Hopes were high – the Sharps Rifle Manufacturing Company is said to have paid $80,000 for the rights – but the seal did not solve the gas-leak problem. Fortunately, a major improvement had soon been made by the gunsmith Richard Smith Lawrence (1817–92).

After briefly serving in the US Army, Lawrence had joined the gunmaker Nicanor Kendall (1809–61); by 1843, he had become Kendall's

This .52-caliber Sharps M1863 Carbine, no. C22331, was issued on February 2, 1865 to Private Amos Hodges of Company C, 15th New York Cavalry. Federal records reveal purchases of 80,512 Sharps carbines between January 1, 1861 and June 30, 1866, but many thousands more were purchased by militia units and individual volunteers and it is suspected that total production approached 150,000. (Morphy Auctions, www.morphyauctions.com)

Elias Warner, born in 1836 in Albany, New York State, enlisted in Company H, 10th US Cavalry on November 1, 1861, re-enlisted on the last day of 1863, and was mustered-out of service on June 26, 1865. He is armed with a Sharps "slant breech" carbine with a set trigger, and an imported saber. Though the Sharps' breech remained prone to gas leaks, which varied in intensity from gun to gun, Sharps firearms were popular with soldiers and civilians alike as they were strong, simple, and reliable. Consequently, they were issued to a wide range of cavalry units. Carbines, if available, were preferred – but full-length rifles armed men in Colorado, Illinois, Indiana, Iowa, Kansas, Kentucky, Maine, Michigan, Minnesota, Missouri, New York, and Pennsylvania, as well as the 2d US Cavalry (Coates & McAulay 1996: 82). (US Library of Congress, Washington, DC)

partner. Kendall & Lawrence became Robbins, Kendall & Lawrence in 1844, but the aging Kendall sold his share in 1847. Robbins & Lawrence thereafter grew rapidly, obtaining a contract to equip the British Royal Small Arms Factory at Enfield with machine tools and then orders for British Enfield rifle-muskets. Although based in Windsor, Vermont, Robbins & Lawrence opened a second factory in 1852 in Hartford, Connecticut, when they successfully tendered to make Sharps firearms. The factory was purchased by the Sharps Rifle Manufacturing Company when the Robbins & Lawrence enterprise failed in 1854. The Lawrence gas seal was patented in December 1859 and, by 1860, the US Marine Corps was optimistically reporting that troubles afflicting the Sharps Carbine had been corrected. The underlying problem was eliminated only by converting caplocks to fire metal-case cartridges after the Civil War had ended, however.

Although 9,141 Sharps rifles were purchased by the Federal authorities in 1861–66, including some for mounted riflemen, carbines were preferred. Sharps' name appeared on the barrel, with an acknowledgment of Lawrence's patent pellet feeder on the lock plate. A cut-off allowed the use of standard percussion caps when necessary. The vertical-breech New Model Sharps of 1859 still fired combustible cartridges, with bases nitrated to facilitate ignition, and had external sidehammers. Most of the M1859 carbines made prior to 1862 had brass furniture, but this was then was replaced by iron. The M1859 was superseded by the New Model Carbine of 1863, clearly marked MODEL 1863 on the barrel. The patch box was abandoned in the spring of 1864 to simplify production, but few other changes were made.

The Burnside carbine

Ranking after the Sharps in popularity was the .54-caliber Burnside carbine, patented in Britain before protection had been granted in the United States in 1856. A few first-type Burnsides were acquired for prolonged US Army trials before the Civil War began. A severe economic depression hit the New England firearms industry particularly badly in the fall of 1857, however, forcing the inventor Ambrose Everett Burnside (1824–81) to sell his patents to creditors, but new proprietors headed by Charles Jackson formed the Burnside Rifle Company in May 1860. Tooling began in a new factory in Providence, Rhode Island, and fresh approaches were made to the US Army even before war began. When hostilities commenced, therefore, the company was well placed.

In July 1861, Chief of Ordnance Ripley passed Jackson an order for 800 Burnside carbines requested by Governor William Sprague IV of Rhode Island on behalf of his cavalrymen. The order was accepted with alacrity, delivery being promised for the end of 1861. The first bulk deliveries are said to have been made in October 1862, work continuing until the perfected or fifth-type Burnside appeared in 1864. A patent granted in July 1863 to gunsmith George R. Bacon had added a pin in the frame to follow a cam-track in the side of the breech block as the action closed. This shut the breech in a single motion; the breech block of .54-caliber Hartshorn (fourth-type) carbines (named after Isaac Hartshorn (1804–77), sales agent for the Burnside Rifle Company) had to be tipped shut manually before the operating lever was closed, but the mechanism would jam if the firer attempted to close the breech before the block had been moved. Carbines embodying the Bacon improvements display MODEL OF 1864 on the frame.

The Burnside carbine remained popular with the Federal authorities until the end of the Civil War, possibly owing to its caplock ignition. Total purchases, 55,567 in 1861–66, ranked it behind only Spencer and Sharps. Burnside carbines were being carried by some of the men of Brigadier General Green Clay Smith's 4th Regiment of Kentucky Volunteer Cavalry captured by Brigadier General Nathan Bedford Forrest's Confederate cavalry after displaying considerable courage during the battle of Brentwood on March 25, 1863. Others were used during the battle of Brandy Station (also known as Fleetwood Hill) on June 9, 1863; at Gettysburg on July 1–3, 1863; and on Brigadier General

THE BURNSIDE REVEALED

.54-caliber fifth-type or M1864 Burnside Carbine

Prototype second-type Burnside carbines tested by the US Army in February 1860 lacked the side-mounted breech latch of the prewar guns. They were operated simply by depressing the combination operating lever/trigger guard patented in April 1860 by George Pratt Foster (1810–74), foreman machinist in the Burnside Rifle Company's Providence factory. A spring-loaded latch was added inside the front of the trigger-guard bow to keep it closed. The third-type Burnside carbine, introduced late in 1861, had a sturdier hammer and a short wooden forend held to the barrel by an iron band.

1. Butt plate
2. Butt
3. Lock plate
4. Barrel band
5. Barrel
6. Front sight
7. Fore stock
8. Sling swivel
9. Hammer (cocked)
10. Hammer (firing position)
11. Breech pin or slider
12. Nipple for percussion cap
13. Flash hole
14. Cartridge block
15. Cartridge in chamber
16. Rear sight
17. Link pivot pin
18. Link
19. Breech bolt
20. Lever-latch post on frame
21. Lever-latch spring
22. Lever latch
23. Operating lever/trigger guard
24. Trigger

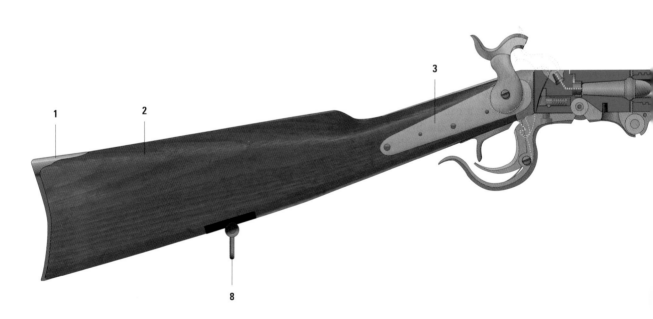

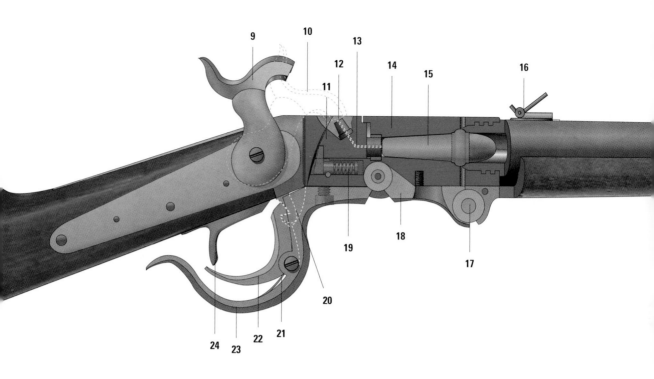

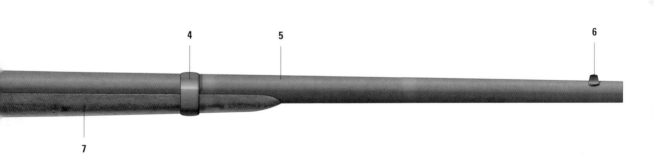

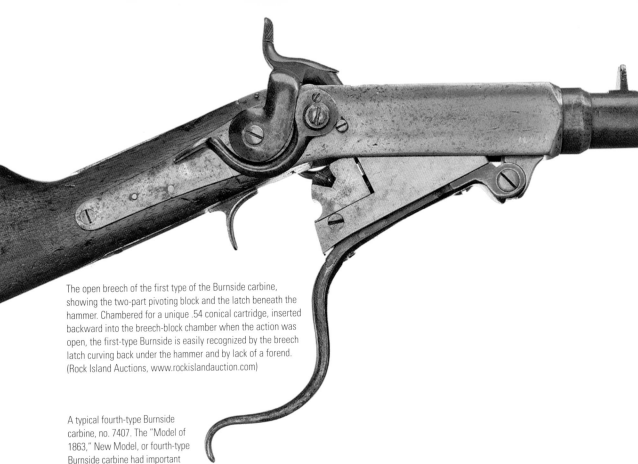

The open breech of the first type of the Burnside carbine, showing the two-part pivoting block and the latch beneath the hammer. Chambered for a unique .54 conical cartridge, inserted backward into the breech-block chamber when the action was open, the first-type Burnside is easily recognized by the breech latch curving back under the hammer and by lack of a forend. (Rock Island Auctions, www.rockislandauction.com)

A typical fourth-type Burnside carbine, no. 7407. The "Model of 1863," New Model, or fourth-type Burnside carbine had important changes in the breech. The comparatively small projection of the open breech block above the frame had made loading difficult, especially on horseback, but an improvement credited to Isaac Hartshorn – usually listed as Burnside's sales agent, but later treasurer and then president of the Burnside Rifle Company – was deposited in May 1862, though the granting of a patent was delayed until March 1863. Adopting a double-pivot breech block and readily detachable hinge pin allowed the block to rise and then tip backward, facilitating loading. (Morphy Auctions, www.morphyauctions.com)

(later Major General) William Tecumseh Sherman's Atlanta Campaign of May–September 1864 and the March through Georgia in November–December 1864.

The Smith carbine

Patented in August 1856 by physician Gilbert Smith, the .50-caliber Smith carbine tested at Washington Arsenal in the spring of 1860 was praised for its simplicity and an unusually gas-tight breech. An order for 300 guns, to allow field trials to be undertaken, had been placed with Poultney & Trimble of Baltimore, Maryland, assignees of Smith's patent, shortly before the Civil War began. Poultney & Trimble then obtained a large order from the Federal government. This was immediately subcontracted, however, to the Massachusetts Arms Company of Chicopee Falls. Production

proceeded satisfactorily until, in August 1863, the Massachusetts Arms Company, preferring to concentrate on the potentially more lucrative Maynard carbine, passed part of the work to Philos Blake Tyler's (1817–76) American Machine Works in Springfield, Massachusetts. Poultney & Trimble suspected that the Smith carbine was being given a deliberately low priority by the Massachusetts Arms Company, and shifted the entire contract to the American Machine Works in September 1863.

Delivered from January 1862 onward, Smith carbines are known to have been carried by the 10th New York and the 1st West Virginia Cavalry at Gettysburg, inventories showing 93 and 81 guns respectively. Other users included Company G, 1st Massachusetts Cavalry during the Union's effort to counter Major General James Ewell Brown "Jeb" Stuart's October 1862 ride around Major General George Brinton McClellan, and the 2d and 4th Indiana Cavalry during the Chickamauga Campaign in Georgia during August–September 1863. Other Union cavalry regiments to use Smith carbines included the 1st Connecticut, 7th and 11th Illinois, 6th and 9th Ohio, 7th and 17th Pennsylvania, and 3d West Virginia.

The .50-caliber Smiths relied on a conventional sidehammer caplock. Some had swivels on the butt and barrel band, but most had a ring-and-bar on the left side of the breech. The guns had been designed to fire a unique rubber-case cartridge, but in December 1863 Thomas Poultney obtained the rights to a patent granted to Thomas Jackson Rodman and Colonel Silas Crispin protecting an improved wrapped-metal cartridge with a strengthening disk or cup. Poultney's Patent Metallic Cartridge, as the Rodman & Crispin design became known, transformed the Smith carbine into a better weapon even though its power was limited by the inherent weakness of the breech-lock bar.

First-type Smith carbine no. 5267 was made in 1862 in Springfield, Massachusetts, by the American Machine Works. The carbines were numbered in separate series, those made by the Massachusetts Arms Company reaching at least 21713 and those by the American Machine Works reaching 18750: total production, therefore, exceeded 40,000, 30,062 of which were purchased by the Federal authorities in 1861–66. (Morphy Auctions, www.morphyauctions.com)

The Starr carbine

The single-shot breech-loading carbine patented by the inventor Ebenezer Townsend Starr (1816–99) had been tested at Washington Arsenal in January 1858, the result of which was the testers' suggestion that it would be a far better weapon than the Sharps carbine if the gas seal could be improved. Accuracy had been impressive, and there had been no misfires. Made by the Starr Arms Company in Yonkers, Binghamton, and Morrisania, New York State, the .54-caliber carbine relied on a two-piece radial breech block with a deep annular recess which, as the action closed, was cammed forward over the barrel by a locking wedge to deflect gas leaks away from the firer's face. The sidehammer caplock worked

satisfactorily as long as the lengthy flash-channel through the nipple was kept clean.

The Ordnance Department ordered 600 Starr carbines in July 1863 and 20,000 in September of the same year. Once a reputation for misfiring had been overcome, the Federal authorities ordered a further 3,000 Starr carbines chambering the .56-52 Spencer rimfire cartridge on February 21, 1865, necessitating a new breech block fitted with an ejector and a modified hammer with a short straight shank. An order for another 2,000, mounted in iron instead of brass, followed within a month.

Federal purchases from the Starr Arms Company amounted to 20,603 caplocks and 5,000 metal-cartridge carbines by June 30, 1866, though few if any rimfire Starrs had been issued. Serial numbers running up to at least 38363, however, show that sales had also been made to individual states. Starr carbines were used by the 2d Missouri Cavalry Regiment (Merrill's Horse) and by other Union Army cavalry regiments including the 1st Arkansas (issued with more than 1,000 in Fayetteville in June 1864), 13th Illinois, 9th Iowa, 5th Kansas, 11th and 12th Missouri, and 24th New York.

The Maynard carbine

The earliest Maynard carbine to be tested officially did not succeed, but a gun tested in Washington Navy Yard in October 1859 placed all of 237 shots on a target 3ft broad by 6ft high at 200yd; at 1,300yd, a significant range for a short-barrel carbine, bullets buried to their length in oak planks. More than 600 shots were fired during the tests, with scarcely a misfire, while two cartridge cases selected at random had each survived more than 100 reloads without failing.

Made by the Massachusetts Arms Company, Maynards were light and handy, weighing only 6.5lb. Though the ungainly straight-wrist butt suggested otherwise, they handled surprisingly well. The breech was opened by pressing down on a lever formed as the trigger guard, tipping the barrel so that a new cartridge could be inserted directly into the chamber. First Model carbines, .35 or .50 caliber, had tape primers. The back sight lay on the tang behind the central hammer, and a saddle ring sometimes lay on the lower tang behind the breech lever. Second Model carbines bought by the Union during the Civil War, however, exclusively in .50 caliber, lacked the tape primer and patch box. They also had a conventional back sight mounted on the barrel above the frame hinge.

Between January 1, 1861 and June 30, 1866, 20,002 Maynards were acquired by the Federal authorities though serial numbers on second-

type carbines run as high as 25215. The alleged purchase, shortly before the Civil War began, of 2,000–2,500 .35-caliber Maynards by the state governments of Florida, Georgia, and Mississippi explains occasional Confederate attributions.

The breech of a .35-caliber Maynard carbine, first type, with the back sight on the butt wrist. Many Maynards of this type were delivered to what became the Confederacy before the Civil War began. (College Hill Arsenal, www.collegehillarsenal.com)

The Gallager carbine

Carbines protected by a patent granted in July 1860 to Delaware-born Dr. Mahlon John Gallager (1814–97) were made in Philadelphia by Richardson & Overman. The barrel moved forward as the breech lever/trigger guard was pressed down, before tipping to give access to the chamber. Though comparatively weak, there was nothing inherently wrong with the action; indeed, many similar designs had been tried

Gallager carbine no. 13366 was made in Philadelphia in 1863 by Richardson & Overman. (Morphy Auctions, www.morphyauctions.com)

successfully in Europe. Gallager, however, had placed half the chamber in the standing breech and half in the barrel. When the gun fired, cartridges tended to stick inside the chamber walls and sometimes ruptured along the circumferential joint between the barrel and the standing breech. The front part of the spent case could stick in the chamber while the rear part was torn clear; or, alternatively, the rear part stuck in the standing breech while the front part was pulled from the chamber. Extraction of cartridge cases was notoriously unreliable, as the special combination tool issued with each Gallager carbine was not strong enough to prize cases free of the breech effectually.

The Federal government, desperate for weapons of any type, acquired 17,738 .52-caliber Gallager caplock carbines in 1861–66; numbers running to at least 23193 suggests that others were sold to individual states. The earliest Gallagers fired combustible linen- or paper-case ammunition, largely superseded during hostilities by Poultney's brass-and-paper or Jackson's paper-wrapped iron-foil cartridges, but they were regarded as greatly inferior to the Burnside, Sharps, and Starr. Gallager carbines were issued to a wide variety of cavalrymen, including the 1st New York, 7th Ohio, 4th Tennessee, and 3d West Virginia regiments. Ordered in March 1865, 5,000 Gallagers chambering the perfected .56-50 Spencer rimfire cartridge were delivered only after fighting had ceased.

Other Federal single-shot cavalry carbines

Statistically less influential designs include Remington carbines embodying the so-called Split Breech, patented in January 1863 by Leonard Geiger (1829–1902). A breech block containing the hammer moved radially in the high-wall receiver, allowing the nose of the hammer to strike rimfire cartridges through a slot in the top surface of the block. The fall of the hammer locked the breech block behind the chamber until the hammer was once again thumbed-back manually. After a successful trial, the Ordnance Department apparently ordered 1,000 Split-Breech carbines chambered for the .44 rimfire cartridge. Remington was preoccupied with revolvers and rifle-muskets, however, so the work was subcontracted to the Savage Revolving Fire-Arms Company of Middletown, Connecticut. A supplementary order placed on January 19, 1865 for 5,000 slightly improved guns chambering a .46 rimfire cartridge was fulfilled only on June 30, 1865 – too late to see service in the Civil War. An order for 15,000 .56-50RF Remingtons had been placed on October 24, 1864, but the last batches were not delivered into store until May 24, 1866.

The .44- and .46-caliber carbines could be identified by their frames, notably smaller than the .56-50 version, and by swivels under the butt and the barrel band. Even low-pressure Spencer ammunition strained the breech mechanism to its limits, however, and so Geiger's Split Breech, though improved in 1863–64 by the gunsmith Joseph Rider (1817–1901), gave way to the Rolling Block.

Baltimore gunsmith James H. Merrill (c.1818–92) initially promoted a .58-caliber carbine designed in partnership with Latrobe & Thomas; made by Remington, 170 were acquired for military trials on July 26, 1855. A patent granted in January 1856 protected the lateral rotarytap or "faucet" breech plug behind the chamber, but the promoters promptly failed. Undaunted, Merrill persevered with Merrill, Thomas & Company until a satisfactory modification of the toggle-type Jenks breech patented in 1838 had been made to accept combustible cartridges. The US Navy was the first to test the .54-caliber Jenks Navy Carbines prepared by the N.P. Ames Company of Springfield; the conversions were approved on January 26, 1861, once a conventional hammer had replaced the original "Mule Ear," but the advent of war halted progress. In June 1861, however, the Union Army acquired a few of the carbines firing regulation-issue paper cartridges or powder-and-ball, ignited by a sidehammer caplock. This design allowed Merrill to claim advantages over the Burnside, Maynard, and Smith carbines which required special cartridges. The action relied on the momentary expansion of an annular copper disk on the piston head to seal the breech as the gun fired. A small lug on the actuating lever automatically cleared the spent cap from the nipple while ensuring that the gun could not fire until the action was fully closed.

Several relevant US patents were granted in 1858–61, and an order for 5,000 Merrill carbines was placed with the Merrill Patent Fire Arms Manufacturing Company of Baltimore on December 24, 1861; manufacture was subcontracted to E. Remington & Sons of Ilion, New York State, whose mark usually appears on the barrel. The earliest carbines of the order had an actuating lever with a flat knurled locking catch, the forend was tapered, and the patch box and fittings were brass. Later carbines had a modified locking catch on the breech lever, embodying a sprung plunger; the forend tip was crude, and the patch box was eliminated. There were also two types of sights. Federal purchases amounted to 14,495 Merrill carbines prior to June 30, 1866; serial numbers on individual guns, however, run to at least 15895.

Benjamin Franklin Joslyn (1825–88), a gunmaker born in Putney, Vermont, was renowned for constant clashes with the Federal authorities. Successful military trials of the first Joslyn carbine, better known as the .54-caliber M1855 "Monkey Tail" carbine – with a lever running back along the wrist of the stock which could be lifted to expose the chamber – had led the US Army to the purchase of 50 examples in November 1857. These .54-caliber Joslyns fired combustible paper cartridges, relying on the momentary expansion of steel rings in the face of the breech to prevent gas leaks.

The US Navy ordered 500 .58-caliber Joslyn rifles in September 1858 though no more than 200 were ever delivered, and the Federal authorities acquired 860 .54-caliber M1855 Joslyn carbines during the Civil War. Often claimed to have been supplied by Bruff, Brother & Seaver of New York, the first 200 seem to have been provided by the W.C. Freeman arms factory in Worcester, Massachusetts, on June 7, 1861 and the remaining 660 by the Joslyn Fire Arms Company of Stonington, Connecticut, in June and July of 1862. Many of the carbines were issued in Ohio early in 1862, 100 going to each division of the 2d, 3d, and 4th US Cavalry regiments and 250 to the 6th US Cavalry Regiment. Brigadier General John Hunt Morgan's Confederate raiders captured many Union men of the 3d and 4th Ohio Cavalry in Lexington, Kentucky, as part of the famous Morgan's Raid conducted in the summer of 1863, allowing Joslyn carbines to fall into Confederate hands.

Joslyn patented a rimfire breech-loader in October 1861. A laterally hinged block or cap, which enveloped the standing breech, could be swung open to the left when the locking catch was released. Cam surfaces were added in 1862, improving cartridge seating and primary extraction, and a patent obtained in August 1863 introduced a riband-spring ejector.

At the end of 1862 a contract for 20,000 rimfire M1862 carbines was acquired, with large-scale deliveries beginning in the summer of 1863, but work was still incomplete when hostilities ceased in April 1865. Made by the Joslyn Fire Arms Company in Stonington, and possibly also by W.C. Freeman, the M1862 carbine chambered .56-52 Spencer rimfire ammunition. The frame had a long upper tang, while the hooked breech cap had a single hinge and the extractor plate was retained by screws. Furniture was invariably brass.

Some of the guns made in 1864 combined the 1862-type action with an improved breech-cap release catch, but they were rapidly superseded by the M1864 carbine. Chambered for .56-52 Spencer or special .54 Joslyn cartridges, the M1864 had a checkered finger-piece let into the underside of the breech hook to reinforce the lock; it also had a cylindrical firing-pin shroud, a gas vent on top of the breech cap, and a short upper tang. Guns numbered above 11,000 also had improved double-hinge breech caps and iron furniture.

When the Civil War ended, the Federal government canceled the incomplete contract, claiming that the Joslyns – 11,261 M1862 and M1864 carbines had been delivered by June 30, 1866 – had failed to meet specifications. Benjamin Joslyn was still complaining long after the war had ended, alleging government duplicity, but problems encountered with his revolvers (many of which inspectors had rejected as unserviceable) suggest poor manufacture to be responsible.

The carbine patented in August 1859 by "Master Gunsmith" Henry Gross (1813–92) had been tested unsuccessfully by both the US Army and the US Navy prior to the Civil War. Pulling the breech lever downward exposed the face of the pivoting breech block, and a separate breech cover dropped to allow a combustible cartridge to be pushed down a loading groove into the chamber. The external caplock had a round-shank hammer. The earliest .52-caliber guns had a serpentine breech lever/ trigger guard with a curled tip which locked in the back of a post beneath the frame.

A contract for 1,140 Gross carbines to arm cavalrymen mustering in Illinois was given on December 23, 1861 to the Cosmopolitan Arms Company of Hamilton, Ohio, a partnership of Edwin Gwyn and Abner Caru Campbell which had acquired the rights to Gross's patent. Once the first order had been fulfilled, Gwyn & Campbell, in October 1862, patented a modified action with a simple grooved breech block dropping at the front to expose the chamber.

The .52-caliber Gwyn & Campbell carbine, also known as the Cosmopolitan Carbine, the Union Rifle, or the "Grapevine" owing to the sinuous breech lever, resembled its predecessor externally. The breech lever locked into the front of the catch-post beneath the butt, however; the hammer sides were flat; and the back sight had been simplified.

Federal purchases totaled 9,342 Gross and Gwyn & Campbell carbines prior to June 30, 1866. At least 4,000 had been issued prior to the end of hostilities: the 5th and 6th Illinois Cavalry regiments taking part in the Vicksburg Campaign of December 1862–July 1863 each had more than 150 of them, the 8th Ohio Cavalry had 900, and the capture on October 20, 1863 of 89 men of the 11th Kentucky Cavalry in Philadelphia, Tennessee, allowed Gwyn & Campbell carbines to fall into Confederate hands.

The Sharps & Hankins Company of Philadelphia arose from antipathy between Christian Sharps and Richard Smith Lawrence, who had a large stake in the Sharps Rifle Company and was responsible – at least according to his own testimony – for most of the improvements

Some of the lesser carbines of the Civil War. Top to bottom: Ball & Williams-made Ballard no. 867, also marked by Merwin & Bray; M1855 "Monkey Tail" Joslyn no. 804, made by A.H. Waters & Company; M1864 Joslyn no. 5549; and Gwyn & Campbell "Union Rifle" no. 4935, made in Hamilton, Ohio. (Morphy Auctions, www.morphyauctions.com)

made in the Sharps action in the 1850s. Consequently, Sharps entered into partnership with Philadelphia merchant and sawmill owner William Hankins to exploit a patent granted in July 1861 to protect a gun with a barrel which slid forward when the trigger-guard lever was pressed. Hankins died before work had got underway, but trading continued and trials of the new Sharps & Hankins guns were successful.

The US Navy ordered 500 rimfire rifles in April–September 1862, chambering the so-called .52 Sharps & Hankins No. 56 cartridge, and special short-barrel carbines armed the 9th and 11th New York Volunteer Cavalry regiments that had been raised in the summer of 1862 – performing well enough to attract the attention of the Ordnance Department, presaging comparatively small-scale purchases on behalf of the Union Army.

Patents granted to the inventor and gunmaker James Warner in 1864 created a .50-caliber carbine whose sturdy cast-brass frame contained a breech block which could be swung to the right to expose the chamber after the thumb-piece near the hammer had been pressed. Extraction of spent cases was then accomplished by retracting a lever protruding beneath the forend. Later guns, made by the Greene Rifle Works in Worcester, Massachusetts, had a sliding breech-block catch – simple and easy to make – on the left side of the frame, accompanied by a sling bar. The first-type sling ring had been held in an eyebolt running transversely through the frame.

A series of small Federal government orders placed in January–November 1864 totaled 1,501 Warner carbines. Unfortunately, the proprietary .50 cartridges often jammed so tightly that they could not be dislodged: the sliding extractor lacked adequate leverage, and spent cases still had to be pulled or shaken from the breech. Consequently, an order for 2,500 Warners which followed on December 26, 1864 was for an improved version accepting the .56-50 rimfire round. The last government Warner carbines were delivered into store in mid-March 1865, by which time some had already been issued: the 1st Wisconsin Cavalry had received 361 when an inventory was taken on March 3, 1865. Warners were also carried by men of the 1st Colorado Volunteer Mounted Militia protecting lines of communication.

Dropping-block rifles and carbines protected by a patent granted in November 1861 to the inventor Charles Henry Ballard (1822–1901) were destined to be made long after many of their contemporaries had been forgotten. The earliest Ballards, made by Ball & Williams of Worcester, Massachusetts, were enthusiastically promoted by Merwin & Bray of New York. The breech block contained the hammer and trigger mechanism, automatically dropping the hammer to half-cock as the action opened.

Designed to chamber rimfire ammunition, Federal-issue Ballards incorporated a supplementary caplock ignition system patented by Joseph Merwin & Edward Bray of New York in January 1864. Seemingly a backward step, this adaptor proved useful when metal-case ammunition ran out. Placing a nipple in the block below the hammer nose allowed a percussion cap to be fired as the neck fell. Combustible cartridges or loose powder-and-ball could be used in emergencies, though, as the breech

was far from gas-tight, better results were obtained by boring a hole in the base of a spent rimfire cartridge which was then loaded with fresh powder and a new bullet. The metal-walled case expanded on firing to seal the breech.

In view of the sophistication of the Ballard design and enthusiastic testimonials, the meager Federal purchases – 35 rifles and 1,509 carbines – are difficult to understand. A contract had been signed as early as October 1862 to supply 1,000 rifles and possibly also 2,500 carbines, but inspectors rejected many of the guns made in Bridgeport, Connecticut, by Dwight Chapin & Company owing to poor quality. A total of 1,600 Ballards were promptly sold to Kentucky, however, where an inventory taken in September 1864 revealed 3,494 carbines and 4,600 rifles to be in service. Perfected Ballard carbines were made by Ball & Williams in .44 or .54 caliber. Most had wooden forends retained by a single barrel band, often bearing a swivel; a second swivel generally lay beneath the butt.

On December 18, 1861, the Ordnance Department contracted with William F. Brooks of New York to make 10,000 of the carbines that had been patented by the inventor and gunsmith Lucius H. Gibbs in 1856. Brooks subcontracted most of the work to the gunmaker William Walker Marston (1822–72), whose Phoenix Armory was situated on the corner of Second Avenue and 22d Street. Marston was bought out on December 1, 1862 by George Opdyke, the Mayor of New York, and deliveries of Gibbs carbines commenced in April 1863. On June 13, however, the Phoenix Armory was destroyed during the New York Draft Riots, Production stopped after only 1,052 .52-caliber Gibbs carbines had been sent into store. An additional 500 were finished and ready for inspection and approximately 6,000 more were in various stages of production when the Phoenix Armory was destroyed.

A lever doubling as the trigger guard tipped the Gibbs carbine's barrel far enough to receive a combustible cartridge. A conventional sidehammer

The Sharps & Hankins carbine, somewhat longer than the so-called cavalry pattern, was often pressed into land service as the Civil War fighting intensified. Note the full-length barrel protector and a carbine carrier attached to a service belt. The carbine had Sharps tangent back sights and a small safety-slide on the rear of the frame which could block the fall of the hammer when appropriate. Navy-issue guns had a leather protector over the barrel to minimize corrosion, held at the muzzle by an iron collar doubling as the front-sight base. Old Models, made in 1861–62, had the firing pin fixed in the hammer face; post-1863 New Models relied on a floating pin in the standing breech. Federal orders were duly placed in 1863, the Union Army eventually receiving 1,468 guns and the Union Navy taking 6,336 from a total which may have exceeded 10,000. (Rock Island Auctions, www.rockislandauction.com)

detonated the percussion cap, flash passing down the nipple channel and out along the axis of a hollow conical spigot which had pierced the cartridge base. An annular collar in the breech face expanded momentarily to act as a gas seal. Gibbs carbines had conventional wooden forends, and could be easily identified by the closed ring on the breech-lever tip.

A carbine patented in March 1859 by firearms designer Edward Lindner (1814–70) was also used officially in small numbers, though alterations of guns for militia or volunteers were more common. A short grasping handle rotated the breech sleeve to the left, allowing the cylindrical breech block to be pivoted upward to receive a combustible cartridge. Ignition was provided by a conventional sidehammer caplock. Some Lindners were converted from imported Austrian Lorenz rifle-muskets, cut to carbine length. Others were assembled from European-made parts and then completed by the Amoskeag Manufacturing Company of Manchester, New Hampshire, though they rarely bore anything other than an acknowledgment of Lindner's patent on the action.

The Federal authorities ordered 400 Lindner carbines on November 6, 1861, to be delivered to Washington Arsenal within eight days. Wartime purchases amounted to a mere 892 first-type carbines, however, supplied "in the white." Used by Michigan cavalrymen during the Second Battle of Bull Run (Second Manassas), fought on August 28–30, 1862, .58-caliber Lindner carbines had a saddle ring and a two-leaf back sight. In April 1863, 6,000 improved Lindners were ordered from Amoskeag, but the Ordnance Department apparently refused to accept them; many were sold in 1870–71 to French agents to serve in the Franco-Prussian War.

The scarcest Federal carbine, judging from Ordnance returns, was patented in 1859–62 by the gunmaker Franklin Wesson (1828–99), younger brother of firearms designer Daniel Baird Wesson (1825–1906). The distinctive frame had two separate apertures, one containing the trigger and the other with the trigger-like latch that released the tipping barrel to expose the chamber. The absence of an extractor meant that stubborn cartridge cases had to be punched out of the chamber with a rod.

Only 151 .44-caliber Wesson carbines were purchased officially from Benjamin Kittredge & Company of Cincinnati, on July 7, 1863, and an additional gun came from Schuyler, Hartley & Graham of New York on August 1. Wesson and Kittredge markings appear on the barrel together, as Kittredge's advocacy ensured that, by 1865, at least 1,366 Wesson carbines had gone to Kentucky and 760 to Illinois. Serial numbers run up to at least 3983.

Principal inspectors' marks usually took the form of initials within a rectangular cartouche. Union marks include HDH (Henry Dewey Hastings, 1833–66) on a Burnside carbine; RKW (Robert Kirkwood Whiteley, 1840–1922) and WHR (William Henry Russell, 1830–86) on a Gwyn & Campbell carbine; TWR (Thomas William Russell, 1833–91) on a Sharps carbine; and GFM (George F. Morrison, 1823–1903) on a Starr revolver. Marks applied by Confederate inspectors include CH of Caleb Huse (usually above "1"), IC of Isaac Curtis, and JS of John Southgate (usually with an anchor) applied to weapons inspected in Britain. (Morphy Auctions, www.morphyauctions.com)

CONFEDERATE-BUILT BREECH-LOADERS

The Robinson carbine

Samuel Couch Robinson (1822–72) – "Merchant, Iron Works" of Richmond, Virginia, according to the 1870 Federal census – was among the Southern industrialists persuaded to make weapons during the Civil War. Output concentrated on a copy of the M1859 Sharps carbine, small quantities of which had been purchased for the Georgia militia shortly before secession occurred. The Lawrence primer was abandoned, while the hammer was not only noticeably slimmer but no longer set into the side of the breech. At least 2,000 carbines of this pattern are said to have been made by December 1862, marked S.C. ROBINSON ARMS MANUFACTORY on the lock plate, together with the location and the date. The government then took control, continuing production or possibly just assembling parts for several months. Marks were eventually reduced to RICHMOND VA. on top of the barrel, with the serial number on the lock-plate tail.

The Morse carbine

A US patent granted in October 1856 to the inventor George Woodward Morse (1812–88) protected a breech-loader firing one of the first metal-case cartridges to be successful in North America. Improved in June 1858, the breech block could be swung up and back around a transverse pivot at the rear, once a catch beneath the forend had been pressed. A carbine had been tested successfully enough by the US Army in 1857 for the conversion of 2,000 muskets to be authorized in September 1858, but progress was slow: only 60 guns had been completed and 540 partly completed when the production machinery was moved in July 1860 to Harper's Ferry Armory. Confederate forces seized the Armory in April

This Robinson-made copy of the Sharps carbine is believed to have been used by Private Lewis Samuel King, who enlisted in Company G, 4th Virginia Cavalry on July 31, 1862. Although the Robinson carbine was the most common of the designs made in the Confederacy, the highest known number, 2458, highlights the weakness of the Southern states' manufacturing industries. Consequently, the Confederate cavalrymen were forced to rely on imports, British P1856 cavalry carbines among them, and the shotguns that had far greater significance in the South than the North. (Morphy Auctions, www.morphyauctions.com)

A typical second-pattern or Type II Morse carbine, no. 333. The first-pattern or Type I Morse carbine has an iron rod in the operating lever to lock the action and, when driven forward by the hammer, to cause a movable firing pin to strike the cartridge primer. Type II Morse carbines – numbered from 200 to about 350 – incorporate a flanged iron rod connected to an iron plate, with knurled edges, which covers the forward upper portion of the brass operating lever. Type III carbines, the last to be made in the State Military Works (numbered from 350 to at least 1033), retain the flanged-rod mechanism, but the breech block is made of iron instead of brass. (Morphy Auctions, www.morphyauctions.com)

Westley Richards shotgun. Short-barrel large-caliber "scatterguns" were greatly favored by cavalrymen, especially Confederate, for close-range combat. (Morphy Auctions, www.morphyauctions.com)

1861, and the machinery was moved successively to Nashville and Atlanta before reaching Greenville, South Carolina. As Morse had by then become State Engineer of Louisiana and was sympathetic to the Confederacy's cause, work on his carbines in the State Military Works in Greenville resulted in the delivery of about 1,000 carbines. Many were issued immediately to the South Carolina Cavalry.

Other Confederate cavalry carbines

Bilharz, Hall & Company of Pittsylvania Courthouse, Virginia, made perhaps 100 rising-block breech-loading carbines by September 1862. The business seems to have been a partnership of Candidus Bilharz, a German immigrant from Strausberg who naturalized in Pittsylvania Courthouse in 1859, and businessman George W. Hall, who by 1880 had become the largest "Tobacconist" in Virginia. Their enterprise was apparently funded by Coleman D. Bennett, a rich and influential man listed in 1860 as "Cashier, Savings Bank" and a colonel of militia during the Civil War. The designer of the carbine remains unknown, though English-born Daniel Clement Hodgkins (1806–91), established as a gunsmith and sporting-goods supplier in Macon, Georgia, in 1832, is a candidate. The challenge of making breech-loaders proved too great, however, and there is no direct evidence that any of them ever saw service. Early in 1863, Bilharz, Hall & Company turned to a copy of the M1855 caplock carbine made with the assistance of parts supplied from Richmond Armory, Virginia: about 750 are believed to have been made before the operation failed in 1864.

Keen, Walker & Company carbine no. 16, a simple design but made only in small quantities. Lacking a forend, the brass framed weapon relies on a block which pivots upward at the mouth when the trigger guard is pushed down. (Morphy Auctions, www.morphyauctions.com)

The carbine once identified as the "Confederate Perry" is now known to have been made in Danville, Virginia, by Keen, Walker & Company – a partnership of Elisha Keen and James Mackenzie Walker, seemingly backed by landowner William Witcher Keen. Records show that Walker

had served briefly with the 18th Virginia Infantry before being discharged on October 5, 1861, presumably to concentrate on gunmaking. A total of 101 examples of the .54-caliber "Keen, Walker & Company Tilting Breech Carbine" were delivered to Danville Armory on May 10, 1862, followed by 100 in the first week of September and 81 on September 16. Work then ended when Keen, Walker & Company acceded to a request from the Virginia state authorities to help with converting Hall rifles to muzzle-loading.

On February 14, 1863, Jeremiah Holt "Jere" Tarpley (1833–82), who had served briefly with the 27th North Carolina Regiment (Guilford Grays), was granted a patent protecting a breech-loader with a side-tipping breech block. Made for Tarpley, Garrett & Company in J. & F. Garrett's foundry in Greensboro, the .52-caliber carbine had a distinctive red-brass frame and seven-groove rifling. An order was placed for 200, apparently in April 1863, for units mustering in North Carolina. It is not clear, however, whether all the carbines had been delivered by the date specified, September 1863, as quality was poor and substantial numbers of those that had been delivered were duly rejected by inspectors.

IMPORTED CARBINES IN CONFEDERATE SERVICE

Federal records note the purchase of 200 "French carbines" and 10,051 "Foreign carbines" in 1861–65, and the Confederacy also imported them in large numbers. Many were Austrian M1842 and M1851 caplocks, which were notably compact, together with substantial quantities of British .577-caliber P1856 cavalry carbines. There were also breech-loaders, though numbers are difficult to assess. They included Terry carbines imported from Britain, and possibly also some of the 12mm French Manceaux Vieillard cavalry carbines discarded after trials in France against the experimental 13.5mm Chassepot type ended in 1864.

The bolt-action system patented by William Terry in April 1856 and improved by Henry Calisher, was obtained in commercial or military style. The former, generally 26 Bore (.568-caliber), was often half-stocked and decoratively engraved, while the latter – usually the so-called 30 Bore (.539-caliber) "Type II" with a key replacing the rear band and an Enfield-type sight – was stocked to the muzzle. Jefferson Davis and "Jeb" Stuart both owned Terry carbines, and others, perhaps as many as 200, saw Confederate service.

P1856 Enfield cavalry carbine, a Confederate import from Britain. (Morphy Auctions, www.morphyauctions.com)

CAVALRY HANDGUNS IN THE CIVIL WAR

Though the breech-loading carbines are often considered preeminent, revolvers and even single-shot pistols probably contributed more to perpetuating the struggle. Surviving .54-caliber M1819 and M1836 flintlock pistols, often converted to percussion, were pressed into service alongside the .54-caliber M1842 caplock pistol. Numbers were appreciable: about 40,000 M1836 pistols had been manufactured by Robert Johnson of Middletown, Connecticut, and Asa H. Waters of Milbury, Massachusetts; and Henry Aston and (later) H. Aston & Company, also of Middletown, had supplied 20,000 M1842 pistols.

Revolvers came in great variety, in calibers ranging from .28 to .50. Some were purchased by national and state authorities, but even more, particularly the small-caliber personal defense weapons, were purchased by or on behalf of individual soldiers. Consequently, almost any type of handgun dating from 1861–65 can legitimately be found with Federal or Confederate attributions. Civil War images often show individuals with several handguns thrust into their belts, and multi-shot capability was undoubtedly an asset in hand-to-hand combat.

Colt revolvers, copies, and clones

Samuel Colt (1814–62) lived long enough to see the introduction of the .44-caliber New Model Army, or M1860, revolver. A replacement for the aging Dragoons that were still in service, this was little more than the M1851 Navy pattern with a longer grip, the front half of the cylinder enlarged, a change to the frame to accommodate the new cylinder, and a contoured rammer shroud. Shortly after production of the M1860 began, a fourth screw was added through the frame and a small readily identifiable cut was made in the lower face of the recoil shield to accept a detachable shoulder stock. The idea seems to have been to supply a multi-shot replacement for the M1855 pistol carbine issued to cavalrymen. A May 19, 1860 report, made by a board of officers appointed to test the merits of Colt and Remington revolvers under the presidency of Acting Inspector General Joseph Johnston, concluded that "the decided advantages which Mr. Colt has gained for his pistol ... will make the most superior Cavalry arm we have ever had."

Colt Army revolvers were made in several identifiable variants, including nonstandard guns made during the Civil War when specific

This Colt M1860 Army revolver was carried by Private Henry Washington Orndorff, who enlisted on February 17, 1862 in Company K, 7th Virginia Cavalry (Ashby's). (Morphy Auctions, www.morphyauctions.com)

Cooper second-type .31-caliber five-shot double-action Pocket Model revolver no. 3075. The position of the trigger lever immediately distinguishes it from the multitude of Colt copies. (Morphy Auctions, www.morphyauctions.com)

components ran short after the fire that destroyed the Hartford factory on February 4, 1864. Back straps were iron, trigger guards were normally brass, and, ironically, the cylinder perpetuated the maritime battle scene depicted on the Navy Colt. Federal purchases of the M1860 revolver during the Civil War amounted to 129,730.

The .36-caliber New Model Navy Revolver, or M1861, combined the small caliber of the M1851 with the sinuous barrel shroud and creeping rammer; 17,010 were purchased during the Civil War by the Federal Ordnance Department. In addition, .31-caliber 1849-type Pocket Models, the .28- and .31-caliber 1855 or "Root Model" sidehammers, and the .36-caliber New Model Police and New Model Pocket Pistol of Navy Caliber all served in appreciable numbers.

Owing to Colt's success, and eventually to the fire which halted production, many copies and near-copies appeared. Navy or .36-caliber revolvers were made by the Manhattan Fire Arms Manufacturing Company of Newark, New Jersey, ostensibly under a patent granted in December 1859 to gunsmiths Joseph Gruler and Augustus Rebetey to protect the inclusion of safety notches on the cylinder. Colt managed to stop production at the end of 1864, but not before Manhattan had made about 80,000 .36-caliber five-shot revolvers.

The Metropolitan Fire Arms Company of New York, founded late in February 1864 to capitalize on the destruction of Colt's factory, made about 6,000 copies of the .36-caliber six-shot Navy Model and New Model Navy revolvers and about 2,750 based on the .36-caliber five-shot New Model Police revolvers. Most had rammers pivoting in the frame ahead of the cylinder. Guns made specifically for H.E. Dimick & Company of St. Louis often had a depiction of the battle of New Orleans (April 24–28, 1862) rolled into the surface of the cylinder.

Externally similar to the Navy Colt, the .36-caliber revolver patented by the inventor James Maslin Cooper in 1860–63 had double-action lock work betrayed by the curved trigger lever set well forward in the guard. About 100 guns were made in Pittsburgh, with a safety-notch system infringing that of Gruler & Rebetey embodied in the Manhattan revolvers, before Cooper moved to Philadelphia in 1864. Production of .36-caliber six-shot Navy revolvers recommenced, initially with iron guards and straps before brass was substituted. The short, smooth-surface cylinder was soon replaced by a double-diameter pattern, the frame being cut away to accommodate the new cylinder. At the same time, the barrel lug was changed to admit conical-ball ammunition.

Marks found on Cooper revolvers include acknowledgments of patents granted in 1851–63 to the gunsmith Stanhope Walker Marston (1802–81) for the lock of a double-action pepperbox; to the gunsmith Josiah Ells (1806–85), protecting the extension around the cylinder-axis pin; and to Charles Harris to protect a modified cylinder-locking bolt.

Remington revolvers

Accounting for 39 percent of Federal revolver acquisitions in 1861–66, Colts were only marginally more numerous than those purchased from E. Remington & Sons of Ilion, New York State (35 percent). The .44-caliber six-shot single-action Remington Beals Army Revolver was a sturdy, solid-frame gun with a rammer protected by a patent granted to the firearms designer Fordyce Beals (1806–70) in September 1858, a brass trigger guard, an octagonal barrel, and a small web beneath the rammer shaft. Unlike later Remington Army revolvers, the attaching threads were invisible where the barrel abutted the cylinder face. Generally blued, with case-hardened hammers, only about 2,000 had been made (alongside 15,000 smaller .36-caliber Navy revolvers) when a rammer patented by the gunsmith William H. Elliot in December 1861 replaced the Beals type. The change supposedly permitted the cylinder-axis pin to be withdrawn without releasing the rammer catch, but the cylinder catch sometimes slid forward on firing and jammed the mechanism.

Excepting the rammer, the 1861-type .44-caliber revolver was practically indistinguishable from the preceding Beals type. Virtually all 19,000 of them were purchased by the Federal government, displaying inspectors' initials in a cartouche on the butt. About 7,500 .36-caliber Navy revolvers were made in the same number sequence, while many .31-caliber New Model Pocket (with a sheath trigger) and .36-caliber New Model Police Remingtons were purchased by individuals.

An improved rammer patented by the gunsmith Samuel Remington (1819–82) in March 1863 replaced the ineffectual Elliott type. The New Model Army Revolvers had safety notches between the nipples and attachment threads visible where the barrel abutted the cylinder face. They also had brass trigger guards, NEW MODEL on the octagonal barrel, and the walnut grips usually bore inspectors' marks.

The box-lid of this Remington New Model Army Revolver, no. 40132 of the Civil War period, bears the marking "Guard. 1." From 1863 until June 30, 1866, Remington supplied the Federal government with 125,314 .44-caliber New Models, constituting almost the entire production run. Each gun cost the Treasury only $13.02, compared with $17.70 for the M1860 Colt. About 23,000 .36-caliber New Model Navy Revolvers had also been acquired prior to June 30, 1866. (Morphy Auctions, www.morphyauctions.com)

The .44-caliber Starr M1858 double-action revolver no. 2437, cased with accessories, was sold privately. What appears to be the trigger, but is actually a cocking lever, had to be pressed to rotate the cylinder mechanically. If the sliding stop on the back of the cocking lever was upward, the gun could be fired simply by continuing the pull: at the end of the stroke, the cocking lever struck the sear release set into the rear of the trigger guard and tripped the hammer. With the cocking-lever stop downward, the hammer remained cocked until the firer released the cocking lever and consciously pressed the sear release. Though achieved at the expense of complexity, this hesitation-cocking action, which may have been influenced by the English Tranter double-action revolvers, released the hammer with far less effort than simply pulling through on the cocking lever. In addition, if a loaded chamber was suitably aligned, thumb-cocking the hammer and then pressing the sear release fired the gun. (Morphy Auctions, www.morphyauctions.com)

Starr revolvers

By June 30, 1866, 47,952 idiosyncratic Starr revolvers had been purchased by the Federal authorities, representing 13 percent of all revolvers acquired during the Civil War. Based on a patent granted to the gunmaker Ebenezer Townsend Starr (1816–99) in January 1856, the .36-caliber version elicited impressive testimonials from antebellum government trials; and Lieutenant Colonel Alexander of the Cavalry Bureau opined that the .44-caliber double-action version was the best revolver for Army use.

Federal purchases of Starrs included 1,000 .36-caliber revolvers for the US Navy in 1858 and then about 1,250 for the US Army, the first authenticated issue being to the 7th Regiment, New York National Guard in April 1861. A .44-caliber version was introduced late in 1861, more than 23,000 being purchased in 1862–63. A simplified .44-caliber single-action Starr, however, incorporating elements of patents granted to Starr in December 1860 and Thomas Gibson in April 1864, was developed to reduce costs and accelerate production. Much of the work was subcontracted to Savage, allowing more than 30,000 guns to be made by the war's end. At least 20,000 were issued to Union forces, each costing merely $12 compared with $25 for the double-action version.

The .44-caliber Starr single-action revolver no. 37935, a simple and sturdy gun which cost the Federal Treasury appreciably less than a Colt M1860. Though not generally as well made as the Colts, Starrs were well liked by those who used them. Their cylinders and axis pins were forged integrally, thus reducing the chance of cap fragments or propellant jamming or fouling the cylinder, and adequate clearance was provided around each nipple. They could be reloaded simply by unscrewing the transverse bolt at the top rear of the frame, allowing the barrel to move forward to release the cylinder. Federal government procurement by June 30, 1866 amounted to 47,952. (Morphy Auctions, www.morphyauctions.com)

Whitney revolvers

The success of Colt persuaded inventors, manufacturers, and entrepreneurs alike to compete in the hope of profit. Consequently, a wide range of revolvers, often short-lived designs, saw service – officially and unofficially – during the Civil War.

The Walker-pattern Colt had been made in the Whitneyville Armory in New Haven, Connecticut, and this persuaded the gunsmith Eli Whitney, Jr. (1820–95) to make revolvers of his own even though hamstrung by the extension of Colt's 1836-vintage master patent. A ring-trigger revolver patented in August 1854 had a one-piece frame with an integral top bar, but Whitney neglected to claim novelty in the solid frame and lost the chance to make a fortune in royalties. Only a handful of these revolvers were made, production instead concentrating on the .31-caliber "Walking Beam Whitney" ring-trigger revolver patented in 1856 by Fordyce Beals and relying on an oscillating bar to rotate the cylinder, and then on the .36-caliber Belt (or Navy) Revolver which proved to be among the more popular revolvers to serve during the Civil War. At least six variants of this weapon have now been catalogued; changes included the addition of safety notches between each pair of nipples, a maritime scene rolled into the cylinder surface, substitution of a rammer-locking wedge for the spring-loaded ball, and five- instead of seven-groove rifling.

Federal purchases of six-shot Whitney Navy revolvers, made in New Haven, Connecticut, amounted by June 30, 1866 to 11,214 for the Union Army; 6,226 for the Union Navy; and 920 acquired in 1863 for the New Jersey State Militia, 792 of which were almost immediately sold to the Army. The highest serial number recorded to date is 30650. Similar revolvers will be found, however, with the marks of W.W. Marston, to whom Whitney probably supplied ready-engraved cylinders and other parts. Others marked by the Union Arms Company and the Western Arms Company were probably assembled after the hostilities had ended.

The first 1,500 Whitneys lacked a rammer, but this was added when the frame was strengthened. Federal purchases, usually numbered in the 15000–25000 group, were of this improved type with a maritime battle scene added to the eagle, shield, and lion that had been rolled into the cylinder surface. Regiments known to have used Whitneys include the Union's 21st Pennsylvania Cavalry, mustered in February 1864, and the Confederate 4th Virginia "Black Horse" Cavalry; "Jeb" Stuart carried no. 3110.

North & Savage and Alsop revolvers

The .36-caliber six-shot revolver patented by Henry S. North in June 1856 was made by Edward Savage and then by North & Savage of Middletown, Connecticut, until an improved version was patented jointly in 1859–60. It had an octagonal barrel, a saw-handle grip, a centrally hung hammer, and a ring-tipped actuating lever protruding below the trigger. A spur-like protector ahead of the operating lever gave the appearance of the figure 8, which the guns are generally classified.

One brass-frame Savage was tested by the US Army Ordnance Department in June 1856, and 100 more were delivered in the late spring of 1857. Next came a variant with an iron frame and a creeping rammer patented by North in April 1858. The third variation reverted to a brass frame, though its sides had been flattened and the spur on the back strap was rounded. A few fourth-type guns, with a flat iron frame and an improved cylinder adjuster, were made in 1860–61. Pulling back on the operating lever revolved and cocked the hammer; releasing it allowed a wedge to press the cylinder forward until the chamfered chamber mouth rode over the end of the barrel to provide an effectual gas seal.

The US Navy ordered 300 Savage revolvers in July 1858, and a 500-gun US Army order soon followed, but deliveries were painfully slow. Total production of "Figure 8" Savages scarcely exceeded 2,000.

The improved 1859-patent revolver, made by the Savage Revolving Fire-Arms Company (successor to North & Savage), shared the general lines of its predecessor except that extending the trigger guard to the base of the butt earned it the sobriquet "Heart Guard." The Massachusetts legislature bought 285 of these .36- or "navy-caliber" revolvers almost as soon as the Civil War fighting began, and others were sold through dealers such as Schuyler, Hartley & Graham. The Union Navy ordered 800 Savage revolvers on May 7, 1861, and an Ordnance Department contract followed on October 16, 1861 requesting delivery of 5,000 guns by the end of March 1862. The Chief of Ordnance, Brevet Brigadier General Ripley, regarded the Savage as "not such a one as I would supply, unless in case of emergency," but another 5,000-gun order was placed in November 1861.

The Federal government had purchased 11,284 Savage Navy Revolvers by June 30, 1866, with another 1,126 going to the US Navy, but production may have ceased once Savage began to make .44-caliber revolvers under contract to the Starr Arms Company in 1864. Savages are known to have been issued to Federal cavalrymen in Illinois, Kansas, Kentucky, Missouri, Ohio, Pennsylvania, Vermont, and Wisconsin, and to Confederate units in Texas and Virginia. Inventories made in 1865 revealed the 2d Wisconsin Cavalry to have 400 of them, while the 4th Missouri Militia Cavalry had no fewer than 714.

The .36-caliber six-shot North & Savage Heart Guard revolvers shared the effectual gas seal of their Figure 8 predecessors, and indexed their cylinders unusually precisely. Fitted with pivoting rammers instead of the original "creeping" pattern, they were both sturdy and durable, though many inexperienced users damaged the lock by attempting to pull the ring lever and the trigger together – the ring lever had to be pulled to rotate the cylinder and cock the hammer before the trigger was pressed. A few guns were made to accept shoulder stocks, patented specifically for mounted use by Charles Alsop in May 1860 and Edward Savage in April 1861.

Alsop revolvers were sheath-trigger diminutions of the perfected North & Savage pattern, made elsewhere in Middletown under protection conferred by patents granted to Charles R. Alsop in 1860–62. A rotary cam pressed the entire cylinder forward over the breech

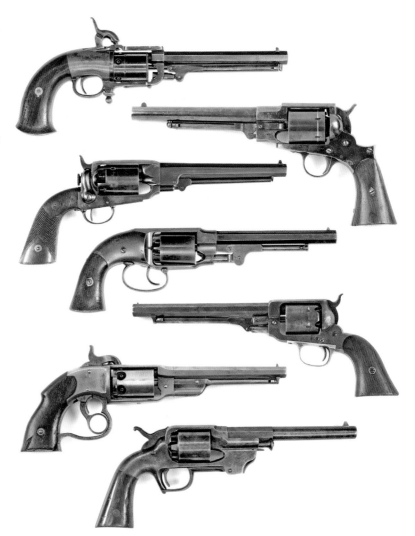

as the elongated hammer spur was thumbed back, supplemented by movable chambers patented by Charles H. Alsop in November 1861. Only about 500 .36-caliber six-shot Alsops were made, however, before work stopped in 1863 in favor of a .31-caliber derivative.

Other Union revolvers

About 2,500 .44-caliber revolvers were made by Charles Brooks Hoard's Armory of Watertown, New York State, to the 1862-patented designs of Austin T. Freeman of Binghamton, New York State. A cylinder-axis pin/locking catch assembly could be pulled forward to disengage the frame and allow the entire cylinder to be taken out of the left side of the gun. Hoard received a Federal government contract for 5,000 revolvers on May 8, 1864, but the largely unfulfilled contract then passed to Rogers & Spencer of Willow Vale, New York State. .44-caliber six-shot Freeman single-action revolvers had a distinctive angular frame and grip. The earliest examples had a detachable side plate; later guns had solid frames with fixed pivot screws for the hammer and trigger.

Charles S. Pettengill of New Haven, Connecticut, received a patent in July 1856 to protect a revolver in which, as the trigger was pulled, a top-mounted cam, assisted by a combination lever patented by Thomas Austin in October 1858, revolved the cylinder and placed the mainspring under tension. When the cylinder had been indexed, the trigger cam disengaged the sear from the hammer and the gun fired.

Rogers & Spencer began to make small-caliber Pettengills in 1859, then obtained a Federal contract for 5,000 .44 ("army caliber") revolvers on December 26, 1861. Simplified in accordance with a patent granted to Edward Raymond and Charles Robitaille in July 1858, they were simply enlargements of the .34-caliber "navy model." Samples failed inspection and an attempt was made to cancel contract, but, after modifications had been made, a 2,000-gun order was placed on June 27, 1862. By January 17, 1863, 2,001 Pettengills had been delivered. Rejections had been high, perhaps one gun in eight, but sufficient numbers were accepted for issues to be made to volunteer cavalry regiments in Arkansas, Illinois, Kentucky, and Missouri.

The .36-caliber Rogers & Spencer revolver, which incorporated as many Pettengill parts as possible, was a conventional six-shot single-action caplock with a shoulderless black-walnut butt giving a cramped appearance. Delivered into Federal stores in January–September 1865, at a cost to the US Treasury of $12 apiece but too late for service, they were subsequently sold to Francis Bannerman & Sons of New York for 25 cents each.

A patent granted in May 1858 to Benjamin Joslyn claimed novelty in a ratchet-type cylinder-rotating mechanism. The .44-caliber five-shot single-action Joslyn had a solid frame, a three-piece rammer, and a side-mounted hammer which allowed the cylinder-axis pin to enter from the rear of the frame. W.C. Freeman contracted with the Chief of Ordnance Ripley on August 28, 1861 to provide 500 Joslyns at an extortionate $25 apiece. Nondelivery caused the contract to be terminated, however. Freeman claimed that he had refused to deliver an "unserviceable design" to the Union Army. A subsequent offer to provide revolvers was declined partly because Freeman's asking price was too high, but largely because 225 Joslyns had been purchased from distributors Bruff, Brother & Seaver of New York in the winter of 1861. Active service revealed serious faults, and many of the unwanted 1,100 guns that had been acquired by the Federal Ordnance Department were passed to the Ohio State Militia at the end of 1861.

Joslyn subsequently made another 2,500 guns in Stonington, Connecticut, with iron trigger guards. Approximately 875 were delivered to the Federal government in 1861–62 and 500 were acquired by the Union Navy, displaying anchors on the butt-strap or under the barrel. An attempt was made in 1862 to sell 675 Joslyns to the 5th Ohio Cavalry but, in light of previous experience, the offer was speedily refused.

The archaic-looking revolver patented by the gunmaker Jesse Butterfield in 1855 had a detachable tube, ahead of the trigger guard, which placed an individual disk primer above the nipple each time the external hammer was cocked. Butterfield accepted a contract for 2,280 .44-caliber five-shot Army Model revolvers placed on behalf of the First Ira Harris Guard of the 5th New York Cavalry, but this was revoked by the Ordnance authorities on June 24, 1862 after only about 700 had been completed by John Krider & Company of Philadelphia. Many Butterfields subsequently found their way to the Confederacy in circumstances which have never been explained.

Protected by patents granted to the gunmaker Ethan Allen (1808–71) in 1857, the solid-framed Allen & Wheelock revolver had some excellent features, not least being the precision with which it indexed its cylinder: a bar placed transversely in the recoil shield, rotated by the hammer, engaged a groove cut across the rear face of the cylinder to turn the next chamber into line. Variants ranged from tiny double-action bar-hammer guns to the perfected .44-caliber Army Model. The sidehammers were cranked to clear the cylinder-axis pin, which entered through the rear of the frame, and the rammer formed part of the trigger guard; a spring-loaded rammer latch replaced the original friction pattern shortly after production began. Revised .36- and .44-caliber center-hammer guns with conventional cylinder-axis pins appeared in 1861, the Federal authorities purchasing 536 .44-caliber examples in 1861–62.

Revolvers built in the Confederacy

When war began, there was no tradition of large-scale gunmaking in the Southern states – even though machinist Abel Shawk (1814–73), possibly backed by farmer Jackson "Jake" McClanahan, had made a small quantity of revolvers based on the Navy Colt. Testimony to the parlous nature of Confederate ordnance is provided by German-born Alfred Kapp (1836–73), who had worked briefly for Colt. After enlisting in the 26th Texas Cavalry Regiment in the summer of 1862, working on farmland owned near Sisterdale by his father Ernst, Alfred Kapp supervised the construction by a small group of German-Americans of at least six somewhat Dragoon-like revolvers.

Enlistees were encouraged to bring any weapon – from flintlock pistols to the latest revolvers – and attempts were made to convert old military flintlocks to caplock. Production of firearms was actively encouraged, but the easiest way of avoiding time and expense lost while developing new designs was to copy something well established. As far as handguns were concerned, this proved to be the .36-caliber six-shot Navy-type or M1851 Colt. Numerically, the greatest contribution to the Confederate armory was made by Griswold & Gunnison of Griswoldville, Georgia, where at least 3,600 .36-caliber six-shot Navy-type revolvers were made until the winter of 1864. The history of these guns remains uncertain, as 80–100 may have been made by New Hampshire-born Arvin Nye Gunnison (1824–82) prior to the evacuation of New Orleans in April 1862. Gunnison subsequently testified that he had removed his machinery to Griswoldville, near Macon, where Samuel Griswold (1790–1867) had created a prosperous cotton-gin manufactory. Griswold was already making swords, sabers, and pikes for the Georgia state authorities.

Confederate .36-caliber Leech & Rigdon Navy revolver no. 693, patterned on the M1851 Colt Navy. (Morphy Auctions, www.morphyauctions.com)

With only an occasional iron-framed exception, Griswold & Gunnison Colts have brass frames. Their cylinders were made by twisting iron bars to minimize the effect of flaws, overcoming shortages of steel and a lack of skills among the largely slave-labor workforce. The earliest guns suffered structural problems – cracked frames were not uncommon – but the strengthened second type was more successful.

English-born Thomas Leech (1826–1908) formed the Novelty Works in Memphis in June 1862 intending to make edged weapons. Threats from the Union Army forced a move from Tennessee to Columbus, Georgia, in May 1862 and then to Greensboro in November. At about the same time, Leech and his new partner, machinist Charles Rigdon (1821–66), accepted a government order for 1,500 .36-caliber Colt-type revolvers. Production began in Greensboro in March 1863, and perhaps 1,000 had been made when the partnership dissolved in December.

Leech seems to have returned to cotton broking, but may have assembled about 100 guns from parts remaining after the split. Rigdon moved the production machinery to Augusta, Georgia, taking merchant Jesse Ansley (1826–1902) as a partner, and work on the 500 guns outstanding from the 1862 contract was completed – the earliest incorporating Leech & Rigdon components – before another order could be accepted. Augusta Arsenal recorded delivery of 903 revolvers between September 1863 and March 1864, 814 of which were subsequently issued for service after passing inspection. Rigdon & Ansley revolvers had six more cylinder stops than the Leech & Rigdons, the ball-type rammer-catch gave way to a Colt-like latch, and a cap-release groove was milled in the recoil shield.

Tucker, Sherrard & Company of Lancaster, Texas, contracted with the state authorities in April 1862 to make 3,000 Colt-type revolvers. Deliveries had not even commenced when Laban Tucker (1806–82) withdrew to form L.E. Tucker & Sons in nearby Weatherford. There he made at least 80 revolvers based on the Navy-pattern Colt. James Taylor, a farmer who had made his fortune in the 1849 Gold Rush, is thought to have joined Joseph Sherrard to form Taylor, Sherrard & Company in the hope of completing the contract. The Dragoon-like .44-caliber guns included a small batch with distinctive low-spur hammers, but output was meager: the highest serial number noted is 129 though, after the war ended, Clark, Sherrard & Company are said to have completed another 300–450 guns.

The Whitney-type .36-caliber Spiller & Burr revolver, shown with its holster and waist-belt, was made only in small quantities – this is no. 13 of the first type, delivered in April 1863. (Morphy Auctions, www.morphyauctions.com)

Founded by James Dance (1823–96) with his brothers George, David, and Isaac, Dance & Brothers of East Columbia and then Anderson, Texas, made .36-caliber Navy, .44-caliber Dragoon, and even .44-caliber Navy-type Colt copies in 1863–64. Apart from the earliest .36 and a handful of .44 examples – possibly made in East Columbia – they lacked recoil shields, conserving raw material by allowing smaller forging billets to be used and thus saving machine time. Production is estimated to have been only about 375, with .36 revolvers predominating.

Comparatively small contributions came from the Augusta Machine Works, where about 100 Navy Colt copies with octagonal barrels and six (rare) or 12 cylinder-stop notches were made, and from the Columbus Arms Company. Founded in 1862 by Prussian-born brothers Louis (1828–71) and Elias Haiman (1843–1914), Columbus made swords and bayonets in quantity before copying the .36-caliber Navy-type Colt in 1863. Most guns had octagonal barrels, though a few apparently had the rounded pattern associated with the Dragoon Colts. Only about 100 had been made before the factory was sold to the Confederate government and moved from Columbus to Macon.

Edward Spiller (1825–74) and David Burr (1820–76) made .36-caliber brass-frame copies of the Whitney Navy revolver in a factory established in Atlanta, at the request of the Chief of Ordnance for the Confederacy Josiah Gorgas and supervised by the renowned engineer John Henry Burton. The first 12 guns were submitted for inspection on December 26, 1862, followed by 40 inspected in Macon Armory in April 1863. There were so many failures, however, that the comparatively weak brass frame was soon strengthened, gaining a thicker top strap, and barrel-attachment threads were no longer exposed between the cylinder and frame. A Colt-type rammer latch also appeared. Production of the modified pattern got underway immediately, but the Confederate government purchased the partnership's assets in March 1863 and moved the machinery to Macon in January 1864. At least 1,030 Spiller & Burr revolvers had been completed in Atlanta then Macon by November 1864, when the proximity of Union forces brought work to an end.

Gunsmith Thomas Cofer (1828–85) of Portsmouth, Virginia, made copies of the .36-caliber Whitney Navy revolver with a brass frame and a distinctive spur-trigger. Originally designed to accept a special cartridge patented by Cofer on August 12, 1861, the finalized revolvers accepted conventional combustible ammunition. The state authorities ordered Cofer revolvers for the 5th Virginia Cavalry soon after the war began, 82 being delivered in January and May of 1862; total production is usually estimated at about 100.

Cavalry handguns of last resort

Even though military-caliber handguns had been acquired in great numbers, there were never enough of them to meet ever-growing needs. In addition, many Civil War combatants and, indeed, noncombatants fearful of their security, purchased guns ranging from minuscule single-shot pistols to sophisticated small-caliber revolvers. The smallest patterns – .28-caliber and .31-caliber cap-and-ball, .22-caliber rimfire – did not have enough power to be effectual, and so were comparatively rarely carried by cavalrymen even as backups: a multiplicity of service-type revolvers was deemed preferable, though the .32-caliber rimfire Smith & Wessons proved their utility later in the war.

Single-shot derringers – a term now accepted as generic for all but true Deringer-made guns – included the .41-caliber rimfire National Model No. 1 "Knuckle Duster" made by Moore's Patent Fire Arms Company and its successor, the National Arms Company of Brooklyn, New York, in accordance with a patent granted to Daniel Moore in February 1861. Nationals had sheath triggers and laterally pivoting barrels giving access to the breech, but were sturdy enough to be used as a knuckleduster when required. Multi-shot designs included the break-open Marston .32RF derringer, patented in 1857, with a monoblock containing three rifled barrels and a traveling striker in the frame to fire the barrels sequentially from the bottom upward. Christian Sharps made thousands of "cluster derringers" with four barrels arranged as two rows of two in a block which slid forward once the retaining catch had been released. A rotating striker plate ensured that each barrel fired correctly.

Colt's success also inspired many rivals, though by the time of the Civil War, many of them had disappeared. Wesson & Leavitts, made by the Massachusetts Arms Company, had been based on Edwin Wesson's mechanization of Daniel Leavitt's manually rotated cylinder (1837). Reloading was simply a matter of pressing a cylinder latch, allowing the barrel to be raised until the cylinder could be pulled forward off the axis pin. Fortified by a questionable extension of his master patent until 1857, however, Colt sued the Massachusetts Arms Company for infringement and won. Production of mechanically actuated Wesson & Leavitts ceased in favor of manually indexed .31-caliber Belt Model guns, 200 of which were supplied to

Typical personal-defense derringers: a .32RF four-barrel Starr, a Sharps & Hankins .22RF four-barrel no. 48926, and the Brown Manufacturing Company's .41RF Southerner no. 6271. (Morphy Auctions, www.morphyauctions.com)

SMITH & WESSON: COPIES AND CLONES

Success ensured that Smith & Wesson soon faced infringements of the company's license with Rollin White. Only Remington had approached Smith & Wesson to reach agreement over metallic-cartridge conversions of caplock revolvers, but fewer than 5,000 .44-caliber Remington Army revolvers were ever converted for a .46 rimfire cartridge by substituting a new five-cartridge cylinder for the original six-shot type.

Among the many transgressions were the six-shot .32RF and "Army Pattern" .44RF sheath-trigger revolvers made by the gunmaker Lucius Willson Pond (1826–89) of Worcester, Massachusetts, under a patent granted to Abram Gibson in July 1860. The barrel/cylinder assembly, hinged at the top rear of the frame, was locked by a lever on the bottom strap; the cylinder-stop slots lay toward the front of the cylinder surface; and the cylinder face was recessed in a recoil shield when the action was closed.

The Manhattan Fire Arms Manufacturing Company of Newark, New Jersey, notorious copyists, made six-shot .32RF facsimiles of the Smith & Wesson Model No. 1. The Bacon Arms & Manufacturing Company of Norwich, Connecticut, made infringements, often unmarked, as well as substantial quantities of six-shot .32RF and .38RF "navy" revolvers embodying a swinging cylinder patented by Charles Hopkins in May 1862. Daniel Moore & Company of Brooklyn, New York, made .32-, .38-, and .44-caliber rimfire revolvers based on a patent granted in September 1860 to protect an open-frame design with a barrel/cylinder group which rotated laterally to the right to facilitate loading. Moore revolvers, among the most effectual and easily loaded cartridge revolvers made prior to 1865, had conventional trigger guards and spring-loaded ejecting rods under the barrel.

Pond, Bacon, and Moore were among those sued for infringement, each case predictably resolving in Smith & Wesson's favor. The defendants were, however, allowed to complete guns which had been partly assembled, provided royalties were paid to the owners of the Rollin White patent and suitable acknowledgments were made.

Attempts to evade Smith & Wesson's patent were made by many gunmakers, including Plant's Manufacturing Company of Southington and then New Haven, Connecticut, which exploited patents granted to Willard Carleton Ellis and John N. White in 1859 and 1863 to protect self-contained "cup primer" metal-case cartridges loaded from the front of the cylinder. Fulminate contained in a longitudinal extension of the cartridge case was ignited by the nose of the hammer projecting through a small hole bored in the rear of the chamber. The first .42-caliber six-shot Plant rimfire revolvers resembled the Smith & Wesson No. 1, and proved to be quite

Abolitionists in 1856 by the Massachusetts Kansas Aid Committee and found their way into the hands of John Brown's supporters.

The Springfield Arms Company made revolvers incorporating a hammer-rotated cylinder patented by its superintendent James Warner in July 1851, and a few .36-caliber six-shot Warner Patent Navy Model revolvers made in the mid-1850s survived to serve in the Civil War. Most of them had the two-trigger system dating from 1852; after the hammer had been cocked, pulling the front trigger indexed the cylinder and then pressed the rear lever to trip the hammer. The rammer pivoted on the barrel lug instead of the cylinder arbor, allowing the barrel to be removed without detaching the rammer.

Horace Smith and Daniel Wesson had acquired the rights to a revolver designed by the gunsmith Rollin White (1817–92). The gun was complicated and potentially very ineffectual, but its chambers were bored through the cylinder at a time when caplock revolvers all had "blind" chambers with a closed rear surface into which the flash-channels were bored. Smarting from the damage inflicted by Colt on the Massachusetts Arms Company, Daniel Wesson was well aware that Colt's master patent expired in 1857. In January 1858, therefore, Smith & Wesson announced the .22-caliber seven-shot Model No. 1 rimfire revolver. This tiny weapon was to be a landmark in firearms history even though the method of rotating and indexing the cylinder was inferior to Colt's design. In addition, the No. 1 lacked a safety or half-cock notch on the hammer, causing accidents with loaded guns.

successful. By 1863, however, a sturdier solid-frame version had been introduced. Total production is thought to have approached 8,000.

Revolvers made by Allen & Wheelock and its 1863 successor, Allen & Company of Worcester, Massachusetts, based on the Allen & Wheelock caplocks, had centrally mounted hammers and cylinder-axis pins entering from the front of the frame. Among them were .32-caliber and .44-caliber lip-fire evasions which still had bored-through cylinders.

Toward the war's end, Daniel Moore introduced a .32-caliber six-shot teat-fire revolver with an open-top frame, a sheath trigger and a bird's-head butt, firing 1864-patent Williamson teat-fire ammunition. Ironically, Moore had obtained a patent in 1863 protecting a revolver with a hinged loading gate ahead of the cylinder, but failed to claim novelty in either teat-fire or the insertion of cartridges from the chamber mouth.

Protected by patents granted to Frank P. Slocum in January–April 1863, assigned to the Brooklyn Firearms Company, detachable sliding sleeves or tubes were pushed forward in the cylinder to allow conventional rimfire cartridges to be inserted, then returned to their original position to provide support during firing. A slot cut in each chamber allowed the hammer nose to pass. Lucius Pond exploited a patent granted to John Vickers in June 1862, using separate chambers, lining tubes or "thimbles," containing conventional rimfire cartridges inserted from the front of the cylinder.

Light-frame Plant revolver no. 7468 was made toward the end of the Civil War. Among the many marks found on Plants are those of the Eagle Arms Company of New York; J.M. Marlin & Company of New Haven, Connecticut; Merwin & Bray Fire Arms Company of New York; and Reynolds, Plant & Hotchkiss of New Haven, Connecticut. (College Hill Arsenal, www.collegehillarsenal.com)

When the Civil War began, only about 11,000 rimfire Smith & Wessons had been made. War, however, was transformative: when the licensing agreement concluded with Rollin White ended on the expiry of his patent on April 3, 1869, 271,639 revolvers had been made. The copper cartridge cases could not withstand anything more than 3 grains of black powder. As the .22 bullet weighed a mere 29–30 grains, therefore, the tiny Smith & Wesson revolver was a very poor man-stopper. By 1861, however, technology had advanced far enough to produce a .32 version. Containing 13 grains of powder and a 90-grain bullet, and even though it was prone to excessive fouling, this was a much better than the feeble .22. Six-shot .32-caliber Model No. 2 revolvers were joined in 1864 by the Model No. 1½ – a light .32-caliber five-shot gun filling the gap between the puny No. 1 and the appreciably larger No. 2.

This foliate-engraved .32RF Smith & Wesson No. 2 revolver, no. 14456, was owned by Colonel John Thomas Wilder, commander of the Union Army's renowned "Lightning Brigade." In spite of its small caliber and tiny cartridge, the Smith & Wesson was popular. It was widely favored by officers, who were not normally issued with regulation-pattern handguns, and also by the rank-and-file as a "backup." (Morphy Auctions, www.morphyauctions.com)

USE
Weapons and war

One of 292 "Confederate M1841 Mississippi Rifles" assembled by six contractors in Nashville for the Tennessee state government. Dating from June 1861 through February 1862, they are often ascribed to John Overton, formerly an armorer in Harper's Ferry Armory, who delivered 81 of them. (Morphy Auctions, www.morphyauctions.com)

ARMING AND ORGANIZING THE CAVALRY

When the Civil War began, the Union Army had only five mounted units: two regiments of dragoons, one of mounted riflemen, and two of cavalry. On August 10, 1861 it was decided to rename all these units as cavalry, numbered according to seniority: the 1st Dragoon Regiment, the oldest, became the 1st US Cavalry Regiment ... and the existing 1st US Cavalry became the 4th US Cavalry. A new unit, the 3d US Cavalry Regiment, mustered only on May 3, 1861, became the 6th US Cavalry under the reorganization, joining the Army of the Potomac. Composed of 34 officers and 950 men, the 6th US Cavalry, excepting one squadron, was armed with pistols and sabers. Not until March 10, 1862 were breech-loading carbines issued universally.

A major inhibition to progress was Brevet Lieutenant General Winfield Scott, commander-in-chief of the Union Army, who took the view that cavalry units were too difficult to train – Scott's successor, Major General George Brinton McClellan, suggested a minimum of two years was needed – in what he believed would be a short campaign, and also wasteful of arms and equipment. McClellan had a low opinion of volunteers, whom he preferred to restrict .to scouting and reconnaissance, and was concerned about the lack of suitable horses. The Confederate military authorities, however, took a very different view. This was at least partly due to familiarity with the horse, which was largely alien to Northern culture. In addition, more than half of the US Army cavalry officers immediately switched allegiance to the South on secession. Volunteers also created a variety of mounted units of their own. As the war continued and more progressive ideas prevailed, 272 Union and 137 Confederate cavalry regiments were eventually mustered.

UPDATING OLDER LONGARMS AFTER APRIL 1861

The tradition of arming horsemen with special weapons gave way when the Civil War led to the issue even of full-length rifle-muskets to mounted units. Carbines and short rifles were preferred for obvious reasons, but they were in short supply. Obsolescent Hall breech-loaders were brought back into service, including 1,575 rifles purchased from the Union Defense Committee of New York, and at least 3,520 carbines were retrieved from state armories.

In May 1861, entrepreneur Arthur M. Eastman of Manchester, New Hampshire, tendered to buy 5,000 M1843 Hall-North carbines stored in Frankford Arsenal, Philadelphia and on Governor's Island, New York. Intending to rifle the smoothbore carbines and enlarge the chamber to take standard .58-caliber ammunition, Eastman re-sold the guns to Simon Stevens of New York. On August 5, 1861, Stevens offered them to Major General John Charles Frémont, commanding the Army Department of the West, who was so desperate for firearms that he asked for immediate delivery of the Hall-Norths. Eastman took possession of the carbines on August 8, 1861; they were altered almost immediately by W.W. Marston & Company of New York and the Taunton Locomotive Manufacturing Company of Taunton, Massachusetts, and arrived in St. Louis in the late summer of 1861.

Chief of Ordnance, Brevet Brigadier General James Wolfe Ripley, then drew attention to the anomaly of guns sold on his authority as surplus to requirements for $3.50 apiece being bought back for $22. Congress authorized an immediate investigation, but no collusion was proven even though Frémont was relieved of his command by President Abraham Lincoln on November 2, 1861. What *was* discovered, however, was that Eastman's original offer to rifle and refurbish the guns for $1 apiece had been rebuffed by the Ordnance Department.

The obsolescent weapons had soon been replaced: on December 30, 1862, Federal stores contained 827 M1819 flintlock and 1,592 M1841 caplock Halls, most of the former being in Frankford Arsenal and most of the latter in Washington Arsenal. The Confederate authorities also pressed Halls firearms into service, seizing 121 of them in Florida, 714 in Georgia, and 2,287 in the former US Arsenal in Baton Rouge, Louisiana. Most of these seem to have been M1819 and M1841 rifles, but at least a few were carbines.

Barrels, bands, and trigger guards found in Harper's Ferry in April 1861 were made-up as muzzle-loaders by foundryman John Baker Barrett of Wytheville, Virginia; and, in 1862, the Virginia Ordnance Department authorized Nathan T. Read and John Watson of Danville, Virginia, to convert about 1,000 Halls from flintlock to caplock, now known generically as "Read's Rifles." Similar conversions were made elsewhere in the Confederacy, a new centrally mounted hammer being characteristic.

The so-called Mississippi or "Yager" rifle of 1841 was also pressed into service with cavalry and mounted infantrymen during the Civil War. Developed from the M1803 flintlock, the first rifle to be standardized by the US Army and improved in 1814 and 1817, the M1841 was made not only in Harper's Ferry but also by subcontractors. As output was surprisingly high, thousands of guns survived at the beginning of the Civil War. Many .54-caliber M1841 rifles were converted after 1855 to fire the standard .58 Minié bullet, gaining new long-range back sights which were changed after 1858 to a simpler multi-leaf design. French-type brass-hilted yataghan-blade sword bayonets were added to many of them, though some attached to a conventional barrel-mounted lug; some were attached with two pivoting rings, one on the pommel and the other, with a locking screw, on the crossguard; and a few had a split-ring attachment. A few of the rifles even had socket bayonets which locked over the bayonet lug/front-sight block. Remington would make substantial numbers of a variant of an upgraded M1841 colloquially known as the "Zouave Rifle" or M1863 during the Civil War.

A typical Confederate Hall flintlock carbine conversion to caplock. The M1833 Hall carbine, a smoothbore developed specifically for the Regiment of Dragoons, was the first caplock to be adopted for service by the US Army. It was succeeded by the M1836, the M1840, the M1842, and the M1843. (College Hill Arsenal, www.collegehillarsenal.com)

A recruiting poster for the New York Mounted Rifles. Financial inducements of this type were attractive to many potential recruits. (Author's collection)

When hostilities began, cavalrymen carried sabers, revolvers, and caplock carbines. Lances were issued only sparingly, largely because the US Army lacked the traditions of European establishments in which cavalry not only took distinctly differing forms – cuirassiers, dragoons, hussars, lancers – but also was regarded as the military elite. Even a catastrophe such as the Charge of the Light Brigade during the Crimean War (1853–56) could be seen in some circles as a vindication of offensive spirit instead of a pointer to the future; but others could see that the growing firepower of infantrymen would eventually prevail.

WARTIME EDGED WEAPONS FOR THE CAVALRY

The speed with which mounted units were raised in the first year of the Civil War caught the ordnance authorities unprepared. Consequently, in addition to increasing production of the regulation French-style sabers that had been standardized in the US Army, by recruiting new contractors, tremendous numbers of swords and sabers were imported: obsolescent patterns which had been discarded, others newly made to regulation patterns (such as British P1853 cavalry sabers), and some which conformed with no official pattern. Blades, finished and unfinished, were supplied to be hilted in North America, together with many individual components.

Swordmakers such as the Ames Manufacturing Company of Chicopee Falls, Massachusetts, made M1833 dragoon and both regulation-pattern cavalry sabers, but output was hardly enough to cope with demand. Consequently, the Federal authorities recruited contractors such as Mansfield & Lamb of Forestdale, Rhode Island, makers of textile machinery and tools in peacetime, who made 36,458 M1860 cavalry sabers. Christopher Roby & Company of West Chelmsford, Massachusetts, made about 32,200; Emerson & Silver of Trenton, New Jersey, made 27,060; and the Providence Tool Company of Providence, Rhode Island, made 11,434 (1861–63).

Many ostensibly US-made edged weapons were obtained from wholesalers and distributors with family ties in Germany, however, such as W.H. Horstmann & Sons of Philadelphia and New York, and Henry Boker of New York. Some were assembled from parts, but others were sent from Europe in finished state. Consequently, the marks of many Solingen cutlers can be found. Henry Boker is said to have imported many of the 45,000 cavalry sabers ordered by the Ordnance Department; Ames brought in 10,000 from Germany in 1861 alone, and even Mansfield & Lamb apparently acquired 18,000.

Lacking the extensive production facilities of the Union, though swords and sabers were made in some numbers by Thomas, Griswold & Company of New Orleans and others, the Confederacy imported a far greater proportion of its needs. Consequently, a broad range of European designs can have plausible Confederate attributions. Thousands of edged weapons were undoubtedly lost to the naval blockade, but many got through; from July 1863 until January 1865, 34 cases of British P1853 cavalry sabers reached Wilmington. These were apparently sent by S. Isaac, Campbell & Company of London, though most seem to have been made by Robert Mole & Son in Birmingham.

A large Confederate Bowie knife with attributions to Private Joseph Dinwiddie of Plum Branch, Virginia, a qualified dentist who served briefly with the Charlotte Cavalry (later 14th Virginia) in the summer of 1861 before becoming the regimental physician. The largest of the knives were sometimes substituted for the sword or saber on the grounds that they were better close-combat weapons and far more useful in the field, acting as woodchoppers or even canoe paddles with equal facility. Particularly popular was the Arkansas Toothpick, a heavy dagger with a long tapering blade, said to have been introduced in the late 1830s by James Black of Washington, Arkansas – the apocryphal creator of the Bowie knife. Yet many other observers regarded the large knives as worthless compared with a saber, and the debate was still raging when hostilities ended. (Morphy Auctions, www.morphyauctions.com)

Two knives made by George Wolstenholm of Washington Works, Wellington Street, Sheffield, owner of the I*XL mark from 1826 (though registered only in 1831). As far as knives were concerned, virtually anything of substance could be pressed into service – from adapted tools to purpose-made bowies. The Confederacy had to import large numbers of knives and unfinished blades from established cutlery-making centers such as Sheffield and Solingen to offset the lack of indigenous production capacity. While bayonets were issued with breech-loading rifles such as the Spencer – and also, in greater numbers, with caplocks such as Springfield and Enfield rifle-muskets and their many derivatives – they were of practically no use to cavalrymen armed with short-barrel carbines. (Morphy Auctions, www.morphyauctions.com)

CAVALRY TACTICS: THEORY AND PRACTICE

Colonel Philip St. George Cooke, father-in-law of Major General "Jeb" Stuart, wrote the comprehensive if controversial *Cavalry Tactics, or Regulations for the Instruction, Formations, and Movements of the Cavalry of the Army and Volunteers of the United States*, completed in 1858 but not published until 1862. The authorities chose to ignore the manual, however, largely as it was at variance with Brevet Brigadier General Ripley's jaundiced view of cavalry even though Cooke espoused the value of mounted attacks as the primary purpose for cavalry forces – at a time when others opined that the widespread issue of rifle-muskets, which increased the range of engagement so greatly compared with their smoothbore antecedents, undermined the value of classic cavalry charges. Yet even the most effectual rifle-musket was still a muzzle-loader: not until breech-loaders chambering self-contained metal-case cartridges appeared in quantity did the primacy of the sword and the saber begin to wane.

Though several regiments of lancers were raised, there was no need – and no real enthusiasm – for the lance in North America. Unlike Europe, where such regiments not only flourished but enjoyed elite reputations, the open plains of North America were ill-suited to cavalrymen who depended on speed and comparatively weak defense to press home attacks using only the lance. Consequently, very few noteworthy attacks would be made by lancers during the Civil War, apart from two by the 5th Texas Mounted Rifles Regiment – at Valverde on February 21, 1862, and during the battle of Catlett's Station on August 22, 1862 – and another by the 6th Pennsylvania Cavalry Regiment (Rush's Lancers) at Hanover Court House on May 27, 1862. It has been claimed that Rush's Lancers used lances at Brandy Station on June 9, 1863, but by this time they had been replaced with carbines.

A well-executed cavalry charge could change the course of battle, particularly if carried forward by experienced officers who could keep their men together, ensure that time and ammunition was not wasted while still too far from the line of engagement, and choose the ideal spot to strike. Infantrymen who had not consolidated their position or were already demoralized made good targets, unlike those who were well armed and could remain calm in the face of a charge.

A Confederate saber marked by Thomas, Griswold & Company of New Orleans, but one of many imported from Europe. Among marks found on blades will be those of Solingen cutlers J.E. Bleckmann (bow and arrow), Clemen & Jung (C&J), Friedrich Herder (crossed keys), Samuel Hoppe (a beehive), Carl Reinhard Kirschbaum (a knight's helm), Paul D. Luneschloss (P.D.L.), Schnitzler & Kirschbaum (S. & K.), and Gebrüder Weyersberg (a king's head). (Morphy Auctions, www.morphyauctions.com)

Valverde, February 21, 1862 (opposite)

Early in the afternoon, Captain Willis Lang led men of the 5th Texas Mounted Rifles against Company B, 2d Colorado Infantry commanded by Captain Theodore Dodd. Cheered on by the crews of the Texan field guns and the vanguard of Major Henry Raguet's companies, the horsemen, their 9ft lances tipped with a 12in point, cantered westward before breaking into a gallop. The first volley, fired from a little over 100yd away caused carnage, however, and then – no more than 40yd from the defenders' line – the lancers met a volley of buck-and-ball. The consequent loss of life was greater than any other company in the Confederate Army of New Mexico had sustained prior to Valverde. Some of the attackers, many of them wounded, had turned back after realizing they had no support. Their useless lances were burned that night, replaced by whatever firearms could be located.

The Civil War image of 6th Pennsylvania Cavalry (Rush's Lancers) cavalrymen shows the 9ft Austrian-style lances with which they were originally armed. (Library of Congress, Washington, DC)

At close quarters, soldiers who had been trained to use their sabers, thrusting where possible rather than slashing wildly at heads and shoulders when wounds were not always debilitating, could wreak havoc. Conversely, however, particularly later in the war, infantrymen armed with breech-loaders chambering self-contained ammunition could fire many more shots than the couple of volleys that could be fired from a muzzle-loader while the horsemen approached – even assuming that loading was effectual. Evidence gathered from the Gettysburg battlefield suggested that many soldiers misloaded muzzle-loaders in the heat of battle: not realizing in the commotion that they had not fired, men simply rammed another cartridge home to render their guns useless. Time was of the essence in such situations: at 20mph, cavalry could travel half a mile in just 90 seconds.

EARLY CAVALRY CLASHES

From the outset of war, Confederate forces were driven by charismatic leaders such as Lieutenant Colonel "Jeb" Stuart and Colonel Turner Ashby, "The Black Knight of the Confederacy," who would be killed on June 6, 1862 during the battle of Good's Farm after repelling an attack by the 1st New Jersey Cavalry. The aggressive use of cavalry was not only recognized but also actively encouraged. In the early stages of the war, therefore, Confederate cavalrymen literally ran rings around their Federal opponents. The imbalance may be seen in the rosters of the First Battle of Bull Run (also known as First Manassas) fought on July 21, 1861: only seven companies of Union cavalry took the field, compared with a regiment, a separate battalion, and several independent companies of Confederate horsemen.

The 11th New York Infantry or Ellsworth's Fire Zouaves, commanded by Colonel Elmer Ephraim Ellsworth, a personal friend of President Abraham Lincoln, and renowned as the first Union force to occupy

THE CAVALRY HORSE'S BURDEN

One of the greatest problems the Union Army cavalry regiments faced was the lack of horses and the terrible conditions in which they were kept by soldiers without any knowledge of equine husbandry. In the late spring of 1862, after a week spent fighting in the Shenandoah Valley, Reverend Henry Rogers Pyne of the 1st New Jersey Cavalry related how "with increasing frequency men could be seen to dismount and attempt to lead forward their enfeebled animals, which, with drooping heads, lack-lustre eyes, and trembling knees could scarcely support the weight of the saddles and equipments" (Pyne 1871: 42).

The loss of horses was too great to bear in the long term: a supply problem as serious in its way as the lack of adequate weaponry. Finally, in July 1863, the Federal authorities created a Cavalry Bureau to work in concert with the Army Quartermaster Department to ensure the Union Army had sufficient horses and associated equipment. Welfare concerns were also addressed, with the introduction of the rank of veterinary sergeant, and, where possible, attempts were made to allow injured and exhausted horses to recover.

In the Confederacy, however, cavalrymen were expected to provide their own horses – a method which worked initially, but which became increasingly strained as the war progressed. The availability of horses suitable for military service rapidly declined and, as costs escalated alarmingly, the value of Confederate cavalry as a fighting force was perceptibly reduced.

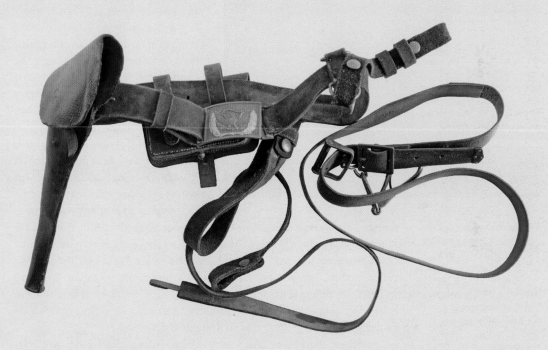

The buff leather M1851 dragoon-saber belt, accompanied by a holster, a cartridge pouch (hidden behind the belt buckle), and a carbine sling. (Morphy Auctions, www.morphyauctions.com)

Spencer M1865 carbine no. 11075, fitted with the Stabler cut-off, is shown with the boot that attached to the saddle. Marks suggest postwar service with the 10th US Cavalry. (Morphy Auctions, www.morphyauctions.com)

This tintype image of a Federal cavalryman dates from the early Civil War period. He is armed with a Hall caplock carbine, an M1840 saber, and an M1860 Colt Army revolver thrust through his belt. (Morphy Auctions, www.morphyauctions.com)

Confederate territory once the Southern states had seceded, backed by men of the 1st Minnesota Infantry, were attacked by 150 of Stuart's cavalrymen while defending Henry Hill. In the confusion, Stuart initially mistook the Zouaves for Confederates – but, after spotting the Union flag carried by a standard-bearer, ordered a section of "Black Horse" cavalry commanded by Captain Richard Welby Carter to charge the Zouaves' rearguard. The New Yorkers carried Sharps carbines, however, and their rapid-fire volleys killed nine of Welby's men before the others fled back into the woods. Though the Confederate charge had had little effect, the Zouaves sustained heavy casualties while covering the Union withdrawal, however.

The battle of Gaines's Mills (also known as Chickahominy River) on June 27, 1862 was renowned for the catastrophic charge of a 237-strong battalion of the 5th US Cavalry, ordered by the cavalry-commander of the Army of the Potomac, Brigadier General Philip St. John Cooke, after the Confederate cavalrymen of Brigadier General John Bell Hood's Texas Brigade had penetrated the Union Lines. The Union cavalrymen were thrown forward to repel Confederate troops in pursuit of Federal artillery as it withdrew; confusion reigned. Charging headlong into merciless fire, the 5th US Cavalry saved the guns but in so doing lost 55 men.

Another charge, on August 9, 1862 during the battle of Cedar Mountain, had comparable results. Conducted by a little over 100 men of the 1st Pennsylvania Cavalry, it had been ordered by Major General Nathaniel Prentice Banks to halt the progress of Confederate infantrymen threatening the Union withdrawal. Protected by picket fences, the infantrymen fired a devastating volley that cost the cavalrymen 30 lives, but enough had been done; the advance halted long enough for Banks's forces to reach to safety.

The battle of Chancellorsville (April 30–May 6, 1863) was remarkable for the huge numbers involved: said to have been 133,868 men of the Union Army of the Potomac against 60,298 of the Confederate Army of Northern Virginia. Cavalry of both armies, commanded by Major General George Stoneman and Major General "Jeb" Stuart respectively, had no great effect on the outcome of a battle which included the bloodiest day in the Civil War after Antietam on September 17, 1862.

USING CAVALRY FIREARMS IN THE FIELD – THREE EXAMPLES

To load the **Spencer carbine**, the cavalryman began by removing the magazine spring and follower – by turning the flange on the magazine tube laterally – and then withdrew the tube through the butt plate. He then dropped seven cartridges into the butt, pointing the gun slightly downward so that they slid toward the front of the magazine. The magazine tube was replaced, pressed home against the resistance of its spring, and the locking flange was rotated back into place on the butt plate. If cartridges were readily to hand, the whole process took perhaps 20 seconds. When he needed to fire, the cavalryman grasped the operating lever, pulling it downward to retract the locking piece and move the breech block radially backward. Closing the lever pushed the first cartridge from the magazine into the chamber and raised the locking piece behind it. The hammer was cocked manually, and pressure on the trigger fired the gun. Re-opening the breech, as smartly as possible, allowed the extractor to push the spent case back over the tongue; the spent case would fall clear. Closing the breech pushed the next cartridge into the chamber, raising the tongue, and the gun could be cocked and fired again. Seven shots could easily be fired in 15–20 seconds if precise aim did not need to be taken.

To prepare the perfected **Burnside carbine** for firing, the cavalryman began by placing the gun at half-cock, then pinched the lever latch between his finger and thumb – or, if experienced, he could push the latch forward with his knuckles – to allow the breech lever to move down and open the breech. A link ensured that the breech block tipped to give access to the chamber mouth, which protruded above the frame. A conical-case cartridge was taken from the pouch, and pushed backward into the chamber. The operating lever was closed until the latch engaged its post. The hammer was drawn back to full-cock, a cap was placed on the nipple, and pressing the trigger fired the gun. Releasing the latch allowed the breech to be re-opened, rotating the chamber upward so that the bell-mouth of the spent case, protruding from the chamber, could be pulled out manually. Another cartridge could be inserted in the chamber, the operating lever was closed, and the firing process began again. Cases were sometimes difficult to extract, owing at least partly to the absence of an automatic extractor, but the Burnside was well liked.

Revolvers were widely issued to cavalry units largely because of their multi-shot capability. To load the **Remington Army revolver**, the cavalryman began by retracting the hammer to half-cock. This allowed the cylinder to revolve freely. Holding the muzzle upward, he then placed black powder and a projectile – usually a lead ball – in an accessible chamber. The cylinder could then be rotated until the freshly loaded chamber aligned with the rammer plunger; the rammer lever was then pulled down, away from the barrel, sliding the plunger back to seat the ball. The process was repeated for the remaining five chambers, and then, if possible, each chamber would be sealed with tallow or any suitable grease-like material. This helped to keep the balls in place, but, more importantly, minimized chain-firing that sometimes occurred when propellant flash traveled radially across the cylinder face to ignite other chambers by penetrating between ball and chamber wall. With the muzzle held down, and the hammer still at half-cock, a cap was placed on each nipple through the cutaway in the recoil shield. The hammer could then be pulled back to full-cock, engaging the indexing pawl, and the revolver would fire when the trigger was pressed. Experienced horsemen sometimes loaded and capped only five chambers, ensuring that the hammer rested on an uncapped nipple. This avoided accidental ignition from a jolt or blow without compromising readiness, as cocking the hammer automatically rotated the next chamber into place. In addition, as the reloading and capping process was slow, and difficult to achieve on horseback, many men carried several revolvers to ensure that fire could be maintained.

M1858 Remington Army revolver no. 48223 was carried by Thomas Morrison of the 18th Virginia Cavalry at battles including Lynchburg (June 17–18, 1864) and Third Winchester (September 19, 1864). (Morphy Auctions, www.morphyauctions.com)

THE TIDE TURNS

The outcome of the battle of Brandy Station on June 9, 1863, just over a month after the battle of Chancellorsville (April 30–May 6) and the first engagement of the Gettysburg Campaign, was very different, however. When the battle began with the 8th New York Cavalry charging across Beverly's Ford, no one knew that the outcome would change the face of the war.

Prior to Brandy Station, Confederate cavalrymen had consistently outmaneuvered and outfought their Union rivals. Though Major General of Volunteers Alfred Pleasonton failed to disperse Major General Stuart's force as he had been ordered to do, and failed to gather intelligence regarding the movements of Confederate forces, he was able to inflict a defeat on his flamboyant rival which began the downhill spiral that was to characterize the performance of Confederate cavalrymen for the remainder of the war. Edward P. Tobie, writing in 1885, quoted Brevet Brigadier General Charles Henry Smith's opinion that the value of Brandy Station to Union success was largely overlooked as the point at which the superiority of Confederate cavalry was finally broken, never to be regained. Smith regarded the battle as the beginning of the end of the war (Tobie 1887: 155).

Reminiscing on his part in the battle of Middleburg (June 17–19, 1863), Private Henry Duxbury, of Company H, 1st Rhode Island Cavalry – armed with Burnside carbines and six-shot revolvers as well as sabers – recalled that "Jeb" Stuart's Confederate cavalrymen:

> … came on the charge, yelling, and some of our own pickets ahead of them. Every one of the ten and our officer stood up without any protection, but the wall, which was hardly any protection whatever. On they came, and so close to us, that we could almost touch some of them with our carbines. We gave them the carbines first and then our revolvers, seventy-six shots in all. As well as I can remember, twice they charged past us to get a fire in their front, when they reached the woods. Here we stayed until another force charged, and halted about two hundred feet up the road. We could hear their officer giving them

The charge of the 6th New York Cavalry during the battle of Brandy Station, June 9, 1863. (Anne S.K. Brown Military Collection, https://library.brown.edu/collections)

orders to form a line, and it looked like they were coming into the field where we were, and Lieutenant Steere gave us orders to follow him and we did so. I do not know how much damage was done by our seventy-six shots, but I have always believed that we helped considerable to close up the Rebellion ... (Bliss 1889: 45)

Officers and men of Company K, 1st US Cavalry, photographed immediately after the battle of Brandy Station. (National Archives, Washington, DC)

A major problem for the Union Army concerned the overly cautious way in which cavalry units were being led, which became important enough for President Lincoln to instruct the commander of the Army of the Potomac, Major General George Gordon Meade, to make whatever changes he considered necessary to galvanize his subordinates. News filtered down to Major General Pleasonton, Meade's cavalry commander. On June 29, 1863, after clearing his ideas with Meade, Pleasonton informed three junior officers of their promotion to Brigadier General of Volunteers: Temporary Staff Captain George Armstrong Custer (then aged 23), Captain Elon John Farnsworth (23), and Captain Wesley Merritt (29), Custer and Farnsworth being attached to Pleasonton's staff and Merritt commanding all 12 companies of the 2d Cavalry Regiment.

The effects were to be far-reaching. It has been suggested that "Jeb" Stuart, smarting from perceived defeat at Brandy Station three weeks earlier, pressed too far northward into Pennsylvania – taking him farther and farther from the Army of Northern Virginia at a crucial moment. His failure to arrive on Gettysburg battlefield in a timely manner had very little effect, compromising General Robert E. Lee's tactics simply by being unable to present reconnaissance in advance. When Stuart's men finally arrived on July 2, 1863, they were almost immediately thrown back by the Michigan Cavalry led by Brigadier General Custer.

The performance of the 6th Cavalry at Fairfield (July 3) against Stuart's two brigades, which were seeking to outflank Union positions in order to attack the supply trains, was a key moment in the battle of

IMPORTED BRITISH REVOLVERS

There were never enough revolvers to meet demand, even in the industrialized North. The Confederacy was obviously far worse off, but the answer was the same: scour Europe for suitable weapons. The manufacture of good-quality revolvers was confined at the time largely to Britain and France, though work was sometimes subcontracted in Belgium where many copyists were at work. Caplock Colts, for example, were produced in quantity in Liége long before the Civil War began. English-made revolvers, in particular, had reached North America in small numbers before the war; often cased and accompanied by a range of accessories, they were usually sold to the wealthy by merchants such as Thomas, Griswold & Company and Hyde & Goodrich of New Orleans.

The Adams revolver and its successor the Beaumont-Adams were preeminent prior to the war, but had had something of a checkered history. The English patent granted to the gunsmith Robert Adams (1809–70) in August 1851 specifically protected a barrel forged integrally with the closed-top frame, which was claimed to be a great improvement over the open-frame Colts which were perceived to be threatening the British market. In addition, the Adams revolver had double-action lock work enabling it to be fired simply by pulling through on the trigger.

Production of the Adams revolver began shortly before the Crimean War (1853–56), and demand grew once the British Army had become interested. A patent granted in February 1855 to Frederick Edward Blackett Beaumont (1833–99) to protect lock work which could be cocked manually, a suitable spur being added to the hammer, was unquestionably an improvement. Even as the Crimean War raged, however, output was relatively small: the English gun-trade was still reliant on traditionally labor-intensive production methods and could not cope with demand. Adams and George and John Deane, his partners in Deane, Adams & Deane of London, licensed the basic design to William Tranter (1816–90) and

Made or perhaps simply assembled by the London Armoury Company, Beaumont-Adams revolver no. 35368R, cased and accompanied by an Alabama Dollar Bill, was retailed by Williams & Powell of 25 South Castle Street, Liverpool. Many blockade runners were built on the Mersey, and it is possible that this revolver accompanied one of them to the Confederacy. (Morphy Auctions, www.morphyauctions.com)

other gunmakers. Sometimes identifiable by serial-number blocks and suffix letters, Adams-type revolvers made by subcontractors may have five-groove rifling instead of three grooves, and some made by Tranter have barrels which screw into the frame.

Robert Adams was one of the promoters of the London Armoury Company, founded on February 9, 1856, but decisions taken to prioritize manufacture of Enfield rifle-muskets had soon persuaded Adams to walk away. The London Armoury Company, after completing Beaumont-Adams revolvers from the parts that remained on hand, apparently with the assistance of Calisher & Terry of Birmingham and Pryse & Redman of London, turned instead to the Kerr revolver.

Adams and Beaumont-Adams revolvers were made in a variety of sizes, but the 54-Bore version, with a nominal caliber of .442, was most common. The original 1854-patent Adams rammer was replaced after 1857 by the Kerr type, patented in 1855, and some guns will be found with Brazier's proprietary design. Serial numbers are generally sequential, even though specific blocks were allocated to other gunsmiths, and patent-royalty numbers will also appear – at least until relevant patents lapsed. Beaumont-Adams revolver 35455 R, dating from 1859, also bears B. 17906.

The US Army had acquired 100 Beaumont-Adams revolvers in 1856 to facilitate trials, persuading the Massachusetts Arms Company of Chicopee Falls to obtain a license to make .31-caliber five-shot Pocket and .36-caliber six-shot Navy revolvers. The last batches of 500 .36-caliber revolvers ordered by the US Army were delivered on September 4, 1858, acquiring the marks of government inspectors William Thornton or Lucius Allin. The state of Virginia purchased 1,000 in May 1860, and about 250 were sold by Schuyler, Hartley & Graham of New York to Alabama shortly before the Civil War began.

Records show that the Federal authorities purchased 415 Beaumont-Adams revolvers prior to June 30, 1866 from the Massachusetts Arms Company. Another 1,075 may have been purchased officially from the London Armoury Company, but many others were acquired by Confederate purchasing agents. The Union 2d Michigan and 8th Pennsylvania, and the Confederate 1st Virginia, 15th Virginia, 16th Virginia, and 5th Georgia Cavalry regiments were among those known to have carried Adams or Beaumont-Adams revolvers.

Statistically, the most important of the Confederate purchases was the Kerr revolver, made by the London Armoury Company in accordance with a British patent granted in December 1858 to Scottish-born gunsmith James Kerr (1822–88). Perhaps 7,000 of about 11,000 Kerr revolvers made in 1859–66 – almost all in .442 caliber – were obtained by Confederate purchasing agents, allowing them to be issued in surprisingly large numbers. Often found with the JS/anchor mark of inspector John Southgate on the

A typical Tranter revolver. This 80-Bore (.387-caliber) example, no. 3997T, cased with accessories, was retailed by Thomas Blissett of South Castle Street, Liverpool, and imported into the United States prior to the Civil War. (College Hill Arsenal, www.collegehillarsenal.com)

grip, numbers run as high as 9974, this being one of seven Kerrs listed by Lieutenant George Julian Pratt on the inventory of Company H, 18th Virginia Cavalry in July 1864.

Patented in February 1853 and initially built on Adams-type frames, Tranter revolvers were also acquired during the Civil War: sold to individuals, often cased, and of the best quality. The earliest Tranter patterns, differing largely in their rammers, embodied a patented hesitation-cocking system in which the cylinders could be revolved and the hammer cocked by pulling back on the spurred cocking lever protruding beneath the trigger guard; pulling the cocking spur and the trigger together gave a form of double action, while single action could be obtained by pulling back on the spur lever and then, separately, on the trigger to trip the sear protruding at the rear of the trigger guard. The so-called Triple Action revolver also had a spur on the hammer which allowed the mechanism to be thumb-cocked when required.

Tranter then produced a much more conventional looking double-action revolver, patented in 1858, though a small rearward projection on the trigger still tripped the sear at the end of its rearward travel. Tranters used in the Civil War would have numbers below 20000T, including "Jeb" Stuart's fourth-type 8673T. Also used in the Civil War in small numbers, often but by no means exclusively by Confederate forces, the so-called "Wedge Frame" Webley embodied a two-part frame locked together by a wedge at the lower front corner. This was intended to circumvent Robert Adams' solid-frame patent while providing more strength than the open frame Colts.

This relic Sharps M1863 carbine, its serial number now indecipherable, was found in Bushman's Woods on South Cavalry Field after the battle of Gettysburg. (Morphy Auctions, www.morphyauctions.com)

Gettysburg. The onslaught of the Union cavalrymen effectively neutralized the Confederate men for much of the day. The 6th Cavalry fought well enough, despite terrible losses, to persuade their opponents that many more men were involved. Otherwise, Stuart's men might have wreaked havoc behind Federal lines.

July 3, the third and final day of the battle of Gettysburg, also hosted the ill-fated Farnsworth Charge, one of the costly attempts to ride down infantrymen who were well placed and confident enough to mount a concerted defense. South Cavalry Field, as it came to be known, saw the Union cavalry charge as the battle drew to a close, conducted by the 18th Pennsylvania, 1st Vermont, and 1st West Virginia Cavalry regiments of Farnsworth's Brigade in an attempt to prevent Confederate General James Longstreet supporting the abortive Pickett's Charge. Though the attack stumbled to a halt, Vermont cavalrymen managed to break through the Texan horsemen screening Confederate infantrymen. The latter were supported by artillery, however, and carnage ensued; Farnsworth fell leading the charge, and his surviving men were forced to withdraw.

THE UNION CAVALRY GAINS THE UPPER HAND

The rise of the Federal cavalry was evident during the epic but somewhat inconclusive battle of Chickamauga (September 18–20, 1863), contested by the Union's Army of the Cumberland under Major General William Starke Rosecrans and the Confederacy's Army of Tennessee under the command of General Braxton Bragg. Though Chickamauga was primarily an infantry battle, there were many occasions on which cavalrymen played important roles. Colonel Wilder's "Lightning Brigade," for example, armed with Spencer rifles, successfully drove their Confederate opponents through "Bloody Pond" on September 20. Conversely, 535 men of the 21st Ohio Infantry, carrying Colt revolver rifles, managed to withstand constant Confederate attacks, many by horsemen, while firing 43,550 rounds. Their heroics, however, played into the hands of those who feared the resupply of weapons and equipment to be impossible in battle. Left behind, out of ammunition, the men of the 21st Ohio Infantry were ordered to fix bayonets; but soon, surrounded by Confederate units, there was no choice but to surrender.

The battle of Yellow Tavern, fought on May 11, 1864 as part of Major General Ulysses S. Grant's seven-week Overland Campaign in May and June, is usually renowned more for the death of Major General "Jeb" Stuart than for the outcome. Major General Philip Henry Sheridan and

Massachusetts Arms Company Beaumont-Adams "Navy Model" revolver no. 342. The .36-caliber revolvers mistakenly show the date of the Adams patent as 1858 instead of 1853, while the .31-caliber revolvers date the patent protecting the Kerr rammer to April 7, 1857 instead of April 14. (Morphy Auctions, www.morphyauctions.com)

his 10,000-strong cavalry force had been detached, however, in an attempt to cut behind General Lee's Army of Northern Virginia.

At about noon, some 4,500 Union horsemen met roughly 2,700 Confederates at Yellow Tavern. The fighting was fierce and prolonged; the Confederate troops defended a ridge for nearly three hours against attackers armed largely with the Spencer carbines that greatly increased firepower. The 1st Virginia Cavalry forced the Union horsemen back, but a dismounted soldier accompanying the retreating 5th Michigan Cavalry shot Stuart with his revolver. The wound was not fatal, even though Stuart's arm was duly amputated, but he died eight days later from pneumonia. The battle had cost the attackers 625 men, killed or wounded, but several hundred Confederate soldiers had been captured and a larger number of Union prisoners had been released.

Trevilian Station, fought on June 11–12, 1864, was not only the greatest cavalry-only battle of the Civil War, but also one that was dominated not by firearms but by the saber. The effectiveness of Federal cavalrymen continued to rise. The Third Battle of Winchester, fought on September 19, 1864, was highlighted by a spectacular charge conducted by more than 10,000 Federal cavalrymen of the Army of Shenandoah, commanded by Major General Sheridan, which sent Lieutenant General Jubal Anderson Early's Confederate troops into panicked flight. A similar

Union and Confederate cavalrymen confront each other (overleaf)

Great use was made of the mobility of cavalry units during the war. Reconnaissance was often the goal, but skirmishes were common and pitched battles such as Brandy Station (June 9, 1863) and Trevilian Station (June 11–12, 1864) involved thousands of horsemen. Here, at the time of Trevilian, men of the 11th Virginia Cavalry under the ultimate command of Major General Thomas Lafayette Rosser confront men of Brigadier General George Armstrong Custer's 6th Michigan Cavalry. The Michigan men are armed largely with M1860 cavalry sabers, M1860 Colt revolvers, and Burnside carbines, though use of Spencer rifles and even a Colt revolver carbine or two testifies to the lack of uniformity found in many regiments. Rosser's men relied more on sabers such as the Virginia Armory pattern than carbines, conferring considerable advantage at close quarters, and carried Colt-type revolvers made either in the Confederacy or captured from Union forces.

rout of Early's men at the battle of Cedar Creek, fought on October 19, 1864, proved to be equally decisive.

The battle of Sailor's Creek, fought on April 6, 1865, was one of the last major confrontations of the war. Among the decisive incidents that brought a Union victory – presaged at the battle of Falling Waters (July 6–16, 1863) and the battle of Five Forks (April 1, 1865) – a massed cavalry charge overwhelmed entrenched Confederate infantrymen who could not, or perhaps would not, face the sabers of their attackers.

IRREGULAR WARFARE AND THE CAVALRYMAN

The role of cavalry was widely seen at the outset of war to be largely one of screening, scouting, and reconnaissance, men often dismounting to fight as rapidly deployable infantry. As fighting progressed, however, the ineffectiveness of traditional cavalrymen away from the set-piece battlefield gave way, at least partly, to long-range raids by what had effectively become mounted riflemen. Wilson's Raid, conducted by Major James Harrison Wilson, commander of the Cavalry Corps of the Military Division of the Mississippi through Alabama and Georgia in March–April 1865, as the war ebbed, involved nearly 13,000 men.

The bloody and lawless traditions of Border Ruffians gave way to the Jayhawkers and the Bushwhackers, exploits such as the devastating raid by William Clarke Quantrill (1837–65) and some 450 guerrilla fighters of Quantrill's Raiders on Lawrence, Kansas, on August 21, 1863 plumbing new depths. Attacking trains, murdering noncombatants, killing livestock, burning homesteads: all were part of the irregulars' lives. No one's property or life was safe, as the Union's Major General James Gillpatrick Blunt noted (Blunt 1932: 239).

The exploits were underwritten by authorities on both sides of the border, sometimes tacitly and at others openly, as the participants were often regular soldiers. One of the most notorious and influential of guerrillas, John Singleton Mosby (1833–1916), commanding the 43d Virginia Cavalry which was destined to become Mosby's Rangers,

Bushwhackers attack a homestead (opposite)

As the Civil War ran its course, guerrilla warfare broke out in Georgia, Kansas, Kentucky, Missouri, Tennessee, and parts of Virginia. Men such as Bloody Bill Anderson, John Mosby, and William Quantrill kept people in fear of their lives, Quantrill's August 1863 raid on Lawrence, Kansas, being one of the best-known atrocities. Here, Bushwhackers attack a stoutly defended homestead. Their clothing and equipment followed no code, so one of the mounted attackers carries a .54-caliber M1841 Mississippi rifle while the man sheltering behind the tree has a British .577 P1856 Enfield cavalry carbine. The other rider brandishes a .44 Remington Army Revolver, a second gun being holstered on his belt, and another can be seen on his mounted colleague's saddle. Revolvers were favored by irregular units, owing to their firepower compared with single-shot carbines. Most men also carried large-bladed knives, which were much more useful than sabers.

IMPORTED FRENCH REVOLVERS

The best-known and perhaps most interesting of the Confederate revolvers was the LeMat, patented in October 1856 by the French-born physician Jean Alexandre François LeMat (1824–95) to protect the substitution of an extra barrel for the cylinder-axis pin and a "gun-cock with double hammer." Protection was also granted in France, Belgium, and Britain, British Patent 1081/62 being granted to LeMat & Girard for improvements that included a spring-bolt cylinder lock.

LeMat was acquainted with Pierre Gustave Toutant-Beauregard (1818–93), destined to be a renowned Confederate cavalry leader during the Civil War but influential enough in prewar days to ensure that a prototype LeMat revolver made by Philadelphia gunsmith John Krider was tested favorably by the US Army Ordnance Department in 1859. Auguste Francotte & Company then made at least 20 Krider-type LeMats in Liége, but the threat of war put an end to the project.

The Confederate authorities gave LeMat colonel's rank and a position in the war ministry on September 21, 1861, and, contemporaneously, contracts for 5,000 "army" and 3,000 "navy" revolvers – all in .42 caliber – were issued. LeMat entered into cooperation with Charles Frédéric Girard MD (1822–95), born in Mulhouse in Alsace, who had been working at the Smithsonian Institution in Washington, DC, when he witnessed LeMat's first patents. Girard accepted a commission from the Confederate government to secure supplies of drugs and medical supplies and left for Paris in the summer of 1861. It is assumed that, in partnership with French-born New Orleans merchant Édouard Gautherin, Girard also accepted the task of gunmaking.

It seems likely that the first LeMat revolvers were made in Liége (or at least assembled from Belgian-made parts) before work was centered in Paris and continued until Girard & Company ceased trading in 1866. Many second-type revolvers have London proofmarks, however, revealing that inspection was undertaken by Confederate representatives in England. There are even largely unsubstantiated suggestions that the revolvers found with Birmingham proofs were made in Britain specifically for the Confederate Navy by Tipping & Lawden of Birmingham.

It has been suggested that only 1,500 LeMats ever reached the South, 900 serving the Confederate Army and 600 with the Confederate Navy, though total production is judged to have been at least 3,000 by 1865. The first consignment apparently reached Savannah in the late summer of 1862, the last known deliveries reaching the Confederacy in July 1864. Guns were undoubtedly lost in unsuccessful attempts to run the blockade of Southern ports, but many simply remained undelivered when hostilities ended.

The Lefaucheux revolver – made in Belgium, France, and Spain in sizes ranging from tiny folding-trigger 7mm to military-type 12mm versions – was protected by a patent deposited in France in June 1854 by Parisian gunmaker Eugène-Gabriel Lefaucheux (1832–92) whose father, Casimir, had patented a pinfire shotgun cartridge in January 1835. Patents of addition granted in 1854–60 ensured the revolvers were exceptionally successful owing to their open-frame simplicity, which kept costs to a minimum, but also to the ammunition. Though vulnerable to discharge if the exposed pin was stuck accidentally, the cartridges were watertight, easy to load, and equally easy to extract.

A Lefaucheux revolver tested by the US Army Ordnance Department in May 1857 was thought to be the "best side-arm for cavalry," but vested interests – the primacy of Colt and prejudice against metal-case cartridges – blocked progress.

Popular with Confederate cavalry officers, the LeMat "Grapeshot Revolvers" were large and heavy. Their rammers and selective-fire hammers were comparatively weak, however, and many guns seem to have failed inspection, yet LeMats gave better service than many other handguns in Confederate service. This first-type example, no. 8, was owned by Confederate General Pierre Gustave Toutant-Beauregard. (Morphy Auctions, www.morphyauctions.com)

LeMat revolver no. 1093, carried during the Civil War by James Mortimer Loudon, who enlisted in 1862 in Company B, 7th Louisiana Infantry Regiment. The essence of the LeMats was an 18-Bore (.637) shot barrel around which the nine-shot .42-caliber cylinder revolved. The first type had an open-top frame and a multi-part rammer carried on the right side of the barrel, conforming to the 1861-vintage French and Belgian patent drawings. A transitional pattern with a rammer pivoting on the left side of the frame led to the perfected type (possibly numbered from 950). The earliest LeMat revolvers have octagonal barrels, though most of the later-type others are half-octagonal. Spurred "cavalry" trigger guards eventually gave way to plain ovals. LeMat revolvers generally share lanyard rings on their butts, lengthy hammer spurs, single-action locks, and a cross pin or spur-type selector on the hammer nose. (Morphy Auctions, www.morphyauctions.com)

When the Civil War began, however, the pinfires were readily available. Union purchases between September 1861 and June 1862 amounted to 11,833 of 11,923 12mm 1854-type revolvers that had been ordered: 9,146 from Eugène-Gabriel Lefaucheux directly, 1,500 from Paris-born but New York domiciled merchant Alexis Godillot (c.1834–1907), 944 from George Raphael & Company, and 333 from six other US-based distributors and wholesalers. All of the revolvers had been made by Lefaucheux, and were numbered between 25000 and 37000. Records also show that 1,856,680 pinfire cartridges were acquired during the war, some of which were made by C.D. Leet in Springfield. Massachusetts.

There were more than enough Lefaucheux revolvers and ammunition to allow issues to Union Army cavalry regiments including the 5th Illinois, 2d and 5th Kansas, 6th Kentucky, 8th Missouri, and 1st Wisconsin, as well as some Missouri militia cavalrymen. The Confederacy acquired perhaps 2,000–5,000 12mm guns, with at least 5,000 less-powerful 7mm and 9mm examples. Also, there can be little doubt that small-caliber Lefaucheux revolvers were also widely purchased by individual Union soldiers.

The Raphael revolver, patented in France in May 1860, was the work of Pidault and Cordier. Martial Pidault, a Parisian gunsmith, had been involved in a variety of gun-related patents granted in France from 1842; Charles Cordier had been involved with Claude-Étienne Minié and also with an 1861-vintage revolver patent. Cordier & Company was granted a license to make "weapons of war" on June 16, 1862, registering an encircled "C.C" trademark on July 14.

The popular name of the revolver comes from that of George Raphael & Company, merchants and commercial agents trading from 109 South Front, Philadelphia, who sold the Federal Ordnance Department 106 9mm six-shot Pidault & Cordier revolvers ordered on September 21, 1861. It has been suggested that Raphael had French connections, though the 1900 Federal census suggests that he had been born in Ireland in August 1820.

The revolver protected by patents granted before 1870 to the gunsmith Louis Perrin (1789–1867), with businesses in Saint-Étienne and Paris, chambered a "thick rim" centerfire cartridge patented in December 1856. The role of co-patentee Delmas, listed as a gunmaker in Paris (but possibly Perrin's employee), is less clear.

The Federal Ordnance Department ordered 1,000 Perrins from the businessman and manufacturer Alexis Godillot (1816–93), the revolvers generally conforming to drawings accompanying the British patent granted in October 1859. The order may not have been placed until 1864, however, as only 550 were ever delivered.

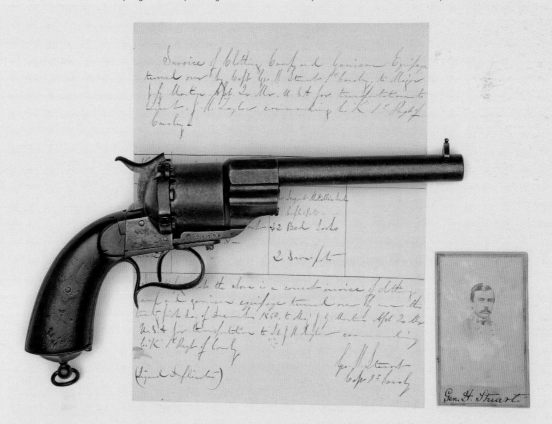

Lefaucheux pinfire revolver no. 28596 was owned by George Hume Steuart, commissioned captain in the 1st Maryland Infantry in 1861 but subsequently serving as brigadier general in the Army of Northern Virginia, commanding cavalry units before returning to infantry duties by the war's end. (Morphy Auctions, www.morphyauctions.com)

Civil War soldier and one-time Quantrill Raider George Webster Maddox with Remington revolvers, one in each hand and a third tucked into his belt. (National Archives, Washington, DC)

recorded that the success of the guerrilla war he was waging could be measured not by the number of prisoners and quantities of war matériel taken from the enemy, but by interfering with lines of communication so greatly that men had to be withdrawn from the front line to protect them. This, Mosby argued, substantially reduced his opponents' fighting strength (Russell 1917: 262).

Not everyone approved of guerrilla tactics, however. On January 11, 1864, Brigadier General Thomas Lafayette Rosser, a senior cavalry officer with a low opinion of partisan rangers in general and Mosby's group in particular, wrote in a letter to General Lee that "… Without discipline, order or organization, they roam … over the country, a band of thieves, stealing, pillaging, plundering and doing every manner of mischief and crime. They are a terror to the citizens and an injury to the cause …" (Official Records 1, 33: 1181). As high-ranking generals, including Lee, broadly concurred, the Confederate authorities disbanded all partisan ranger corps excepting those of Mosby and Captain John Hanson MacNeill (McNeill's Rangers), which fought until the end of the war. Nevertheless, they had played their part.

The weapons carried by partisan raiders and comparable irregular groups, regardless of their political affiliations, rarely complied with regulations. This was partly due to problems of supply, not only of the weapons themselves but also of ammunition. Much of the disputed territory was sparsely settled, and supply lines were often stretched to their limits simply by the demands of regular forces. Obtaining cartridges for breech-loaders, particularly those that required metal-case ammunition, could be impossible. Consequently, guns firing powder-and-ball were preferred. Propellant could be obtained by cannibalizing virtually any type of preloaded cartridge, combustible or self-contained, and, largely owing to the low melting point of lead, projectiles were readily made with the assistance of molds. In desperation, virtually anything that could be loaded could be fired: small pebbles in place of lead balls could work effectually if accuracy was irrelevant.

It is evident from surviving photographs that the most popular firearm was the revolver, individuals often being shown carrying three or more. John Munson confirms that a pair of .44-caliber Colt revolvers were regarded as standard and that sabers or carbines were never used (Munson 1906: 22–23). One obvious advantage was firepower: many of the confrontations were at short range, and the 18 shots that could be fired from three Colt or Remington revolvers conferred a very obvious advantage over the single-shot caplock carbine or even a seven-shot Spencer. Shotguns were also employed in large numbers, largely because they could fire almost anything that could be dropped down the barrel.

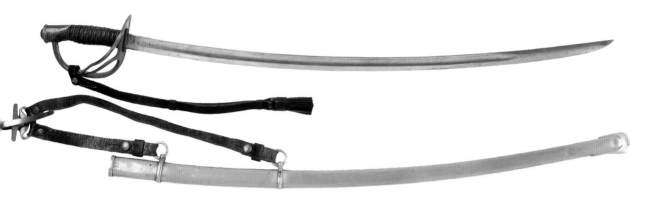

IMPACT
Weapons: fact and fiction

Cavalrymen traditionally relied on single-shot pistols and sabers, quickly supplemented by breech-loading carbines and revolvers, and, particularly in Confederate units, by shotguns and large-bladed knives. Surviving images show individuals armed with several revolvers as well as a saber, knife, and carbine, but there was very little consensus and the advantages of the differing weapons have been disputed ever since.

The rapid growth of mounted units made standardization of weapons impossible, as volunteers on both sides took the field with whatever could be obtained. Some Rhode Island cavalrymen, for example, were armed with Burnside carbines partly for political reasons but also because their manufacturer was based in the same state. The *Annual Report of the Quarter Master General of the State of Ohio for the Year 1862* summarized the weaponry of the state's seven cavalry regiments, the 1st Squadron, and the 2d Independent Battalion as: 500 Gallager, 550 Joslyn, and 864 Sharps carbines; 1,161 Colt, 999 Joslyn, 2,727 Remington, 700 Starr, and 250 Whitney revolvers; and 7,334 sabers, mostly M1860 cavalry sabers. The record for the 4th Ohio Cavalry was noted as incomplete, as all but 100 Joslyn carbines had been supplied by the Federal authorities, and the Joslyn and Sharps carbines of the 5th Ohio Cavalry were replaced early in 1863 by Burnsides.

Each type of weapon had its advantages and drawbacks, thus suiting none of them to universal issue. The needs of well-trained cavalrymen facing similarly effectual horsemen were far removed from those who attacked infantrymen, or the irregulars fighting in wooded uplands far removed from the traditional battlefield. Men who fought at Brandy Station or Trevilian Station, the great cavalry battles of the war, faced very different challenges at Gettysburg, riding with Mosby's Rangers, or taking part in Sheridan's rampages as the war drew to a close.

One of 10,000 M1860 cavalry sabers made in 1861–62 by D.J. Millard & Company, of Clayville, New York State. The M1860 was basically a lightened M1840. (Morphy Auctions, www.morphyauctions.com)

EDGED WEAPONS AND THE CAVALRY CHARGE

The saber retained its champions not only to Appomattox but for decades thereafter, despite the ever-growing popularity of revolvers, shotguns (especially in the South), and repeating carbines, as well as enforced changes of tactics.

There were officers who clung to the belief that a cavalry charge was still a game-changer. Custer was particularly fond of the all-out saber charge, which served him well at Trevilian Station even though such bravado verging on recklessness had endangered his liberty, perhaps even his life, when all-but surrounded at Brandy Station some months earlier. After the Third Battle of Winchester, Custer reflected that his opponents had "relied wholly upon the carbine and the pistol; [while] my men preferred the saber. A short but costly struggle ensued, which resulted in the repulse of the enemy" (quoted in Whittaker 1876: 240).

Others argued that such attacks had had their day. The Union's Colonel John Thomas Wilder armed his brigade with long-handle hatchets, arguing that they were far more deadly than a sword at close quarters, and many believed that sabers – and socket bayonets for that matter – were best used as candelabra or roasting spits. According to one officer:

> The Federal cavalry generally fought with sabers; at any rate they carried them, and Mosby used to say they were as useless against a skillfully handled revolver as the wooden swords of harlequins. As the Mosby tactics became better known, scouting parties from the Northern army began to develop an affection for the pistol, with increasing success I might add. In stubborn fights I have seen the men on both sides sit on their restless horses and re-load their pistols under a galling fire. This was not a custom, however; someone generally ran to cover after the revolvers were emptied. We both did this a good many times but, I believe, without bragging at the expense of truth, that we saw the back seams of the enemy's jackets oftener than they saw ours ... Revolvers in the hands of Mosby's men were as effective in surprise engagements as a whole line of light ordnance in the hands of the enemy. This was largely because Mosby admonished his men never to fire a shot until the eyes of the other fellow were visible ... (Munson 1906: 23–25)

REVOLVER OR SABER?

The revolver was popular among many cavalrymen, largely because of its compact dimensions (it could be used one-handed on horseback) and multi-shot capability. Revolvers were viable only at short range, however, and liable to misfire when the shock of a charge dislodged caps or even bullets within their chambers. In extreme cases, the bullet could project far enough from the chamber mouth to prevent the cylinder rotating within the frame. Reloading a caplock on horseback was difficult, though not impossible, which at least partly explains why men can be seen in

The "Wade Hampton Saber," credited to one of the Confederacy's leading cavalry generals, was distinguished by its heavy double-edged blade, 38in long, imported from Solingen. Made by Kraft, Goldschmidt & Kraft of Columbia, South Carolina, in two patterns – the other has a hilt similar to that of the M1860 cavalry saber – each saber originally had a leather finger-ring attached to the guard to help to swing such a heavy weapon without losing grip. (Morphy Auctions, www.morphyauctions.com)

Civil War photographs with three or more revolvers thrust into their waist-belts.

The advent of handguns chambering metal-case cartridges was a major advance. The Federal authorities issued Lefaucheux pinfires to a broad range of cavalry units, and the comparatively low-powered Smith & Wessons were greatly favored as back-up weapons. Effectual use depended on the availability of sufficient ammunition, however. In an era when transport was slow and unwieldy, and resupply could take weeks instead of days and days instead of hours, units could find themselves deprived of firepower.

Champions of the revolver pointed to the experience of the Confederacy's Lieutenant General Nathan Bedford Forrest, whose men had clashed with Union horsemen near Maplesville, Alabama, on April 1, 1865. Forrest and his men were considerably outnumbered by Union cavalrymen who had ridden furiously at them with drawn sabers. The .36-caliber Navy Colts carried by the Confederates proved their worth, however. Forrest himself sustained a cut to the head from a glancing saber blow, but shot his assailant before more damage could be done. When the skirmish was over, the Confederates claimed that 30 Union cavalrymen had been killed, and many others wounded, at a cost to themselves of six men wounded in addition to Forrest. The day, they said, clearly belonged to the revolver.

Others were not as convinced, however, including Major Floyd Clarkson of the 12th New York Cavalry, who commanded an expedition against Tarborough and Rocky Mount, North Carolina, on July 20, 1863. Charging Confederate cavalrymen, only to be ambushed by dismounted horsemen hiding in woods, Clarkson's inexperienced men wasted the advantages of their revolvers by firing too quickly. The attack failed, but Clarkson, after withdrawing a short distance, ordered sabers to be drawn even though the spirited charge that resulted also proved ineffectual. An inference has been drawn from this and similar occasions that men were not as keen to press home an attack armed with handguns rather

Kerr revolver no. 4239, with its holster. This gun was owned by Edward Rutledge Liles, commissioned as lieutenant in Company B, 31st North Carolina Infantry on October 3, 1861. Promoted lieutenant colonel in September 1862, Liles was mustered-out of service on April 3, 1863. (Morphy Auctions, www.morphyauctions.com)

than sabers; but this often came down simply to the determination of individual officers and lack of adequate training.

LONGARMS: CONTROVERSIAL NEW TECHNOLOGIES

When the fighting began, though trials had been underway with a variety of breech-loaders for many years, the muzzle-loader still reigned supreme in the minds of men such as the Union Army's commander-in-chief, Brevet Lieutenant General Winfield Scott, and the Union's Chief of Ordnance, Brevet Brigadier General James Ripley, whose active service had occurred many years earlier. Initially, despite the scramble to equip countless new regiments, there was no consensus. Many preferred the Sharps to weapons such as the Burnside and the Maynard, largely because, even though the breech leaked gas, the Sharps could fire combustible ammunition or even powder-and-ball loaded from the muzzle – which could be the difference between life and death if cartridge supply failed. Surviving records testify to the widespread issue of breech-loading carbines, virtually all of which had prewar origins. Many of them gave good service in particular localities, such as the Ballards in Kentucky, without ever gaining universal approval.

The advent of the self-contained cartridge and the repeating rifle would change warfare, but not until long after the Civil War had ended. There were simply too few guns to force changes to be made in tactics, despite successes such as that of Wilder's "Lightning Brigade" at Hoover's Gap on June 24–26, 1863, which was widely attributed to the overwhelming volume of fire delivered from Spencer rifles (often mistakenly identified as carbines). The attitude of the Ordnance Department is implicit in the decision by Wilder to purchase the Spencers personally, though each of his men had to sign an indemnity for $30. After the battle, however, the Federal treasury agreed to cover the costs. Wilder, an experienced engineer who had patented hydraulic machinery and a waterwheel, appreciated the potential of the Spencer in a way many high-ranking officers did not.

The Confederate partisan rangers sometimes equipped themselves with carbines captured from Union troops, but many men regarded them as awkward, unhandy, and not as effectual as a revolver. Carbines were long enough to be an encumbrance; difficult to reload in the saddle, they were often used simply as clubs.

M1860 Spencer carbine no. 37413 and 1851 Navy-type Colt revolver no. 93632, shown with holster, made by J.L. Pittman of New York, and cartridge pouch by J. Davy & Company of Newark, New Jersey, were carried by William H. Lovering, who enlisted in the 1st Rhode Island Cavalry on Christmas Day 1861. (Morphy Auctions, www.morphyauctions.com)

CONCLUSION

The surrender of Confederate General in Chief Robert E. Lee at Appomattox Court House on April 9, 1865 effectively brought the Civil War to a close, though sporadic fighting continued until the news reached outlying posts. The armed forces were immediately reduced in size once the Civil War was over, but weapons were still being delivered into store in completion of wartime contracts. Most of these guns, never to be issued, except in small numbers to state militia, were auctioned at a fraction of their cost, often finding their way West with wagon trains and railroad construction crews. Many were traded to the Native Americans, including some which helped to kill Custer and his men at the battle of the Little Bighorn (June 25–26, 1876). Ironically, Custer, a long-time admirer of the cavalry saber, had had to rely on the slow-firing "Trapdoor" Springfield carbines of the 7th US Cavalry instead of the repeating Spencers his Michigan troopers had carried at Brandy Station 13 years previously. This typified the way in which the lessons of the Civil War had been learned. The value of cavalry had been enhanced by experience, no longer being regarded primarily as a scouting force. Yet the cavalryman's weapons remained just as they had been at the start of the war: saber, revolver, and carbine.

The technological revolution had almost bypassed the Ordnance Department, which, led by aging officers whose service went back many years, remained reluctant to endorse progress. Consensus could be found in the replacement of muzzle-loading rifle-muskets with breech-loading rifles, and in the patently obvious advantages of self-contained metal-case ammunition. Yet there were diehards who resisted the universal introduction of such cartridges, arguing that supplying them over vast distances could not be guaranteed: even as the railroad network grew, there could still be hundreds of miles between settlements. Powder-and-ball ammunition was more reliable, they claimed. If breech-loaders were accepted grudgingly, repeating rifles and carbines were viewed with suspicion – an even better way to encourage men to waste ammunition by blazing away unchecked.

Lineal successors to the cavalry carbines of the Civil War: M1873 "Trapdoor" Springfield no. 41826 and the rarely encountered M1895 Krag carbine, no. 27012, few of which were made before the M1896 was substituted. (Morphy Auctions, www.morphyauctions.com)

This photograph of a Union Army cavalry corporal, taken at the end of the Civil War, shows a Spencer carbine and an M1860 cavalry saber. (US National Archives, Washington, DC)

Accepting that improvement in the US Army's small arms was required, the service began lengthy trials to find replacements for the caplock rifle-muskets. In January 1865, several months before peace had been concluded, the submission of breech-loading carbines and rifle-muskets had been solicited to facilitate trials. Eventually, the Ordnance Department, rejecting anything that would involve paying licensing or royalty fees in accordance with an Act of Congress of June 1860, settled on the Allin conversion that had been patented in September 1865. This decision has been widely vilified, but the primary goal was to upgrade stocks of rifle-muskets to breech-loading without unreasonable cost or complexity. This was not uncommon: for example, the British converted Enfields to Sniders, and the French converted a selection of caplocks to the Snider-like Tabatière breech.

The postwar role of US Army cavalrymen became largely one of policing the territories that were rapidly expanding the Union. Manning the forts and keeping Native American depredations at bay became primary concerns. The weapons initially remained largely unchanged, however, perhaps because such vast stores remained. Men made do with M1860 cavalry sabers, Colt M1860 revolvers, Sharps single-shot carbines altered to chamber metal-case cartridges, and – initially at least – Spencer repeaters. The Spencer was comparatively low-powered, however; its .56-50 rimfire cartridge could not compete with the first .50-caliber Allin conversions, and though this was not particularly disadvantageous in the saddle, it was a handicap when men were acting as infantry. Limited range and a slow-moving bullet could easily compromise effectiveness.

Eventually, the US Army's cavalry received a carbine derivative of the .45-caliber M1873 "Trapdoor Springfield" infantry rifle and the new-and-effectual M1873 Colt revolver. Once again, this has been questioned: would Custer have fared better in 1876 if the 7th US Cavalry had been armed with Spencers? The answer is probably "yes," as long as ammunition supplies held out – an important caveat given the numbers of Native Americans involved. Battlefield archeology has undermined persistent claims that the Springfield carbines were unusually prone to jamming, when extractors tore through cartridge rims as the breech opened, but they remained essentially slow-firing weapons.

Experiments were undertaken with supposedly better weapons, including Hotchkiss bolt-action magazine carbines, but Springfields remained the front-line weapons of the US Army's cavalry until approval of the .30-caliber Krag carbine in 1896. Yet the US Army was far from alone in restricting the efficacy of firearms issued to cavalry. The French approved the Berthier *Carabine de cavalerie* only in 1890, and the British, as convinced of the value of the cavalry saber as the US Ordnance Department, issued single-shot Sniders and Martini-Henry carbines until the .303in Lee-Metford Mk I magazine carbine was sealed in on September 29, 1894.

The advent of the Krag magazine carbine finally put the US Army's cavalrymen on the same footing as their European counterparts – but it had been a long and often tortuous path from the Spencer carbine of the Civil War.

This list presents details of some of the principal US patents associated with military firearms used by cavalrymen during the Civil War. The information is presented in date order because patent marks on US firearms – invariably dated – almost never identify the number and only rarely bear the inventor's name. Specifications and drawings can be accessed through the US Patent and Trademark Office website (www.uspto.gov).

1836
February 25, 9430X (Colt revolver; reissued October 14, 1848)

1845
September 22, 4208: Edward Maynard, Washington, DC (tape primer)

1848
September 12, 5763: Christian Sharps, Hartford, CT (Sharps carbine)

1851
January 7, 7887: Stanhope W. Marston, New York, NY (Cooper revolver)

May 27, 8126: Edward Maynard, Washington, DC (Maynard carbine)

1854
April 25, 10812: Josiah Ells, Pittsburgh, PA (Cooper revolver)

1855
January 2, 12124: Jesse S. Butterfield, Philadelphia, PA (Butterfield revolver)

August 28, 13507: Benjamin Franklin Joslyn, Worcester, MA (Joslyn carbine)

December 25, 13999: Elisha Root, Hartford, CT (Colt-Root rifle and revolver)

1856
January 8, 14057: Lucius Gibbs, New York, NY (Gibbs carbine)

January 15, 14118: Eben Townsend Starr, New York, NY (Starr revolver)

March 25, 14491: Ambrose E. Burnside, Bristol, RI (Burnside carbine)

April 1, 14554: Hezekiah Conant, Hartford, CT (Sharps carbine)

June 3, 15032: Frederick Edward Blackett Beaumont, Upper Woodball, Barnsley, England (Beaumont-Adams revolver)

June 17, 15144: Henry S. North, Middletown, CT (Savage revolver)

July 22, 15388: Charles S. Pettengill, New Haven, CT (Pettengill revolver)

August 5, 15496: Gilbert Smith, Buttermilk Falls, NY (Smith carbine)

October 28, 15995: George Woodward Morse, Baton Rouge, LA (Morse carbine)

1857
January 13, 16367: Ethan Allen, Worcester, MA (Allen & Wheelock revolver)

December 8, 18836: Ethan Allen, Worcester, MA (Allen & Wheelock revolver)

1858
April 6, 19868: Henry S. North, Middletown, CT (Savage revolver)

May 4, 20160: Benjamin Franklin Joslyn, Worcester, MA (Joslyn revolver)

June 8, 20503: George Woodward Morse, Baton Rouge, LA (Morse carbine)

July 20, 20954: James H. Merrill, Baltimore, MD (Merrill carbine)

July 27, 21054: Edward A. Raymond and Charles Robitaille, Brooklyn, NY (Pettengill revolver)

September 7, 21400: Ethan Allen, Worcester, MA (Allen & Wheelock revolver)

September 14, 21478: Fordyce Beals, New Haven, CT (Remington-Beals revolver)

September 14, 21523: Eben Townsend Starr, New York, NY (Starr carbine)

October 12, 21730: Thomas K. Austin, New York, NY (Pettengill revolver)

1859
January 18, 22666: Henry S. North, Middletown, CT, and Edward Savage, Cromwell, CT (Savage revolver)

March 29, 23378: Edward Lindner, New York, NY (Lindner carbine)

August 30, 25259: Henry Gross, Tiffin, OH (Gross carbine)

October 25, 25926: Franklin Wesson and N.D. Harrington, Worcester, MA (Wesson carbine)

December 20, 26504: Richard Smith Lawrence, Hartford, CT (Sharps carbine)

December 27, 26641: Joseph Gruler and Augustus Rebetey, Norwich, CT (Manhattan revolver)

1860

March 6, 27393: Christopher Miner Spencer, South Manchester, CT (Spencer carbine)

April 10, 27874: George Pratt Foster, Providence, RI (Burnside carbine)

May 15, 28331: Edward B. Savage, Cromwell, CT, and Henry S. North, Middletown, CT (Savage revolver)

May 22, 28433: Charles Richard Alsop, Middletown, CT (Savage revolver)

July 17, 29157: Mahlon John Gallager, Savannah, GA (Gallager carbine)

July 17, 29213: Charles Richard Alsop, Middletown, CT (Alsop and Savage revolvers)

September 4, 29864: James Maslin Cooper, Pittsburgh, PA (Cooper revolver)

October 16, 30447: Benjamin Tyler Henry, New Haven, CT (Henry rifle)

December 4, 30843: Eben Townsend Starr, New York, NY (Starr revolver)

1861

April 9, 32003: Edward B. Savage, Cromwell, CT (Savage revolver)

July 9, 32790: Christian Sharps, Philadelphia, PA (Sharps & Hankins carbine)

October 1, 33382: William Elliot, Plattsburg, NY (Remington revolver)

October 8, 33435: Benjamin Franklin Joslyn, Worcester, MA (Joslyn carbine)

October 22, 33536: James H. Merrill, Baltimore, MD (Merrill carbine)

November 5, 33631: Charles H. Ballard, Worcester, MA (Ballard carbine)

November 26, 33770: Charles Richard Alsop, Middletown, CT (Alsop and Savage revolvers)

1862

January 21, 34226: Charles Henry Alsop, Middletown, CT (Alsop and Savage revolvers)

October 21, 36709: Edwin Gwyn & Abner Campbell, Hamilton, OH (Cosmopolitan carbine)

November 4, 36861: Henry S. Rogers, Willow Vale, NY (Pettengill revolver)

November 11, 36925: Franklin Wesson. Worcester, MA (Wesson carbine)

December 9, 37091: Austin T. Freeman, Binghamton, NY (Freeman revolver)

1863

January 27, 37501: Leonard Geiger, Hudson, NY (Remington carbine)

March 17, 37921: Samuel Remington, Ilion, NY (Remington revolver)

March 31, 38042: Isaac Hartshorn, Providence, RI (Burnside carbine)

July 21, 39270: George R. Bacon, Providence, RI (Burnside carbine)

August 4, 39407: Benjamin Franklin Joslyn, Stonington, CT (Joslyn carbine)

September 1, 39771: Charles W. Harris, Pittsburgh, PA (Cooper revolver)

September 22, 40021: James Maslin Cooper, Pittsburgh, PA (Cooper revolver)

December 8, 40887: Joseph Rider, Newark, OH (Remington carbine)

1864

January 5, 41166: Joseph Merwin & Edward P. Bray, New York, NY (Ballard carbine)

February 23, 41732: James Warner, Springfield, MA (Warner carbine)

April 19, 42435: Thomas Gibson, Yonkers, NY (Starr revolver)

November 15, 45123: Joseph Rider, Newark, OH (Remington carbine)

December 6, 45361: Louis Triplett, Columbia, KY (Triplett & Scott carbine)

December 20, 45532: Eben Townsend Starr, New York, NY (Starr revolver)

December 21, 45469: Erastus Blakeslee, Plymouth, CT (Spencer carbine)

December 27, 45660: James Warner, Springfield, MA (Warner carbine)

1865

March 14, 46828: Edward Stabler, Sandy Springs, MD (Spencer carbine)

SELECT BIBLIOGRAPHY

Bliss, George N. (1889). *The First Rhode Island Cavalry, Middleburg, Va, June 17 and 18, 1863*. Providence, RI: Rhode Island Soldiers and Sailors Historical Society.

Blunt, James G. (1932). "General Blunt's Account of His Civil War Experiences" in the *Kansas Historical Quarterly*, May 1932, Vol. 1 No. 3: 211–65.

Coates, Earl J. & John D. McAulay (1996). *Civil War Sharps Carbines and Rifles*. Gettysburg, PA: Thomas Publishing.

Gaines, W. Craig (2008). *Encyclopedia of Civil War Shipwrecks*. Baton Rouge, LA: Louisiana State University Press.

Hall, Clark S. (2019). 'The Battle of Brandy Station', available at https://www. essentialcivilwarcurriculum.com/the-battle-of-brandy-station.html (accessed October 20, 2019).

Hicks, Major James E., with André Jandot (1962). *U.S. Military Firearms 1776–1956*. La Canada, CA: James E. Hicks & Son.

Jones, Gordon L. (2014). *Confederate Odyssey: The George W. Wray Jr. Civil War Collection at the Atlanta History Center*. Athens, GA: University of Georgia Press.

Lewis, Berkeley R. (1956). *Small Arms and Ammunition in the United States Service 1776–1865*. Washington, DC: Smithsonian Institution Press.

McAulay, John D. (1981). *Carbines of the Civil War, 1861–1865*. Harriman, TN: Pioneer Press.

McAulay, John D. (1987). *Civil War Breech Loading Rifles. A survey of the innovative Infantry arms of the American Civil War*. Lincoln, RI: Andrew Mowbray, Inc.

McAulay, John D. (2006). *U.S. Military Carbines*. Lincoln, RI: Andrew Mowbray, Inc.

Munson, John W. (1906). *Reminiscences of a Mosby Guerilla*. New York, NY: Moffat, Yard & Co.

Official Records (1864). *The Official Records of the War of the Rebellion, Series 1*. Washington, DC: War Department Publications Office.

Phillips, Gervase (2019). "Sabre versus Revolver: Mounted Combat in the American Civil War", available at https://www.academia.edu/205649/Sabre_versus_Revolver_Mounted_Combat_in_the_American_Civil_War (accessed October 20, 2019).

Pitman, Brigadier General John (1987). *Breech-Loading Carbines of the United States Civil War Period*. Tacoma, WA: Armory Publications.

Pritchard, Russ A. Jr, & C.A. Huey (2015). *The English Connection. Arms, Materials and Support Furnished to the Confederate States of America by Great Britain*. Gettysburg, PA: Thomas Publications.

Pyne, Henry R. (1871). *The History of the First New Jersey Cavalry, (Sixteenth Regiment, New Jersey Volunteers)*. Trenton, NJ: J.A. Beecher.

Russell, Charles W., ed. (1917). *The Memoirs of Colonel John S. Mosby*. Boston, MA: Little, Brown & Co.

Tobie, Edward P. (1887). *History of the First Maine Cavalry Regiment 1861-1865*. Boston, MA: Emery & Hughes.

Walter, John D. (1999). *The Guns that Won the West: Firearms on the American Frontier, 1848–1898*. London: Greenhill Books.

Walter, John D. (2006). *The Rifle Story, an Illustrated History from 1756 to the Present Day*. London: Greenhill Books.

Whittaker, Frederick (1876). *A complete life of Gen. George A. Custer: Major-General of Volunteers; Brevet Major-General, U.S. Army; and Lieutenant-Colonel, Seventh U.S. Cavalry*. New York, NY: Sheldon & Co.

INDEX

Figures in **bold** refer to illustrations.

accessories/accoutrements 8, 9, 13, 36, 37, 54, 55, 60, 60, 74
Adams revolver 60, 61
Allen & Wheelock revolvers 40, 42, 47
Allin conversion (rifle-muskets) 76
Alsop revolvers 39–40
armies, Confederate: Northern Virginia 56, 59, 63; Tennessee 62
armies, Union: Cumberland 62; Potomac 48, 56, 59: Shenandoah 63
Augusta revolver 44
Austria, weapons supplied from 7, 30, 33

Bacon revolvers 46
Ball carbine 14
Ballard carbines 9, 12, 27, 28–29, 74
battles: Antietam 56; Appomattox 72, 75; Brandy Station 17, 52, 58, 58, 59, 59, 63, 71, 72, 75; Brentwood 17; Catlett's Station 52; Cedar Creek 66; Cedar Mountain/Chancellorsville 56; Chickamauga 62; Fairfield 59, 62; Falling Waters 66; First Bull Run 54, 56; Five Forks 66; Gaine's Mill 56; Gettysburg 17, 21, 54, 58–59, 62, 71; Good's Farm 54; Hanover Court House 52; Hoover's Gap 12, 74; Lynchburg 57; Middleburg 58–59; New Orleans 35; Sailor's Creek 66; Second Bull Run 30; Third Battle of Winchester 57, 63, 72; Trevilian Station 63, 64–65, 71, 72; Valverde 52, 53; Yellow Tavern 62–63
bayonets 5, 44, 49, 51, 62, 72
Beaumont-Adams revolvers 60, 60, 61, 63, 63
Bilharz & Hall carbines 32
breech-loading carbines/rifles 5, 6, 8, 9, 48, 71, 74, 75, 76
Britain, weapons import from 7, 33, 51, 51, 60–62, 60, 61, 67, 68
Brown Southerner derringer 45
Burnside carbines 9, 12, 17, 18, 18–19, 20, 20, 25, 30, 57, 58, 64–65, 71, 74
Butterfield revolver 40, 41–42

cavalry charges 54, 56, 58–59, 62, 63, 66
Clark & Sherrard revolvers 43
Cofer revolver 44–45
Colt revolvers 4, 34–36, 34, 35, 37, 42–44, 43, 56, 62, 64–65, 70, 71, 73, 74, 76
Colt-Root revolving carbine 14, 14
Columbus revolver 44
Confederacy (the)
    blockade of Southern ports 7, 7, 51, 60, 68
    weapons imports 7, 31, 33, 33, 51, 51, 52, 60–62, 60, 61, 67, 68, 68
    weapons manufacturing 6, 7, 42–45, 51
Confederate Army cavalry regts 17, 48, 58, 62, 73
    by state: GA 61; LA 68; SC 32; TX 39, 42, 52, 53, 56; VA 31, 33, 34, 38, 39, 45, 54, 56, 57, 61, 63, 64–65, 66
Confederate Navy, revolvers for 68
Cooper revolvers 35–36, 35
Cosmopolitan carbine 12, 27

daggers 51
Dance revolvers 44
derringers 45, 45

Enfield P1856 carbine 31, 33, 33, 67
Enfield rifle-muskets 6, 7, 16, 51, 61

Federal purchases 6–7: carbines 14, 15, 17, 20, 21, 22–23, 24, 25, 26, 27, 28, 29, 30; revolvers 35, 36, 37, 38, 39, 40, 41, 42, 61; rifles 13, 14, 16, 29
flintlocks 6, 9, 42, 43, 49
France, weapons imports from 7, 33, 68, 68
Freeman revolver 40–41, 40

Gallager carbine 12, 23–24, 24, 71
Germany, weapons import from 7, 51, 52, 52
Gibbs carbine 12, 29–30
Griswold & Gunnison revolver 42, 43
Gross carbine 26–27
guerrillas/irregulars, weapons of 26, 66, 67, 70, 70, 71, 72
Gwyn & Campbell carbines 27, 27, 30

Hall carbines 4, 5, 15, 33, 49, 49, 56
Hall-North carbines 49
Hartshorn carbine 17
hatchets 72
Henry carbine/rifle 9, 12, 13, 13
Hoard revolver 40
holsters 43, 55, 57, 68, 73, 74
Hunt rifle 9

inspectors' marks 13, 15, 30, 30, 36

Jenks carbines 15, 25
Joslyn carbine/rifle 12, 25, 26, 27, 71
Joslyn revolvers 40, 41, 71

Keen & Walker carbine 32–33, 32
Kerr revolver 61, 73
knives 51, 66, 71

lances, use of 7, 50, 52, 53, 54
Leech & Ridgeon revolver 43, 43
Lefaucheux revolvers 9, 68–69, 69, 73
LeMat revolvers 68, 68
Lindner carbine 12, 30
Lorenz rifle-muskets 30

Manceaux Vieillard carbines 33
Manhattan revolvers 35, 46
Marston derringer 45
Maynard carbines 12, 21, 22–23, 23, 25, 74
Merrill carbine 12, 25
Metropolitan revolver 35
militia forces, weapons for 14, 15, 30, 31, 38, 39, 41, 69, 75
Moore revolvers 46, 47
Morse carbine 9, 31–32, 31
musketoons 5
muskets 7, 31
muzzle-loaders 33, 49, 54, 74, 75

National derringer 45
North & Savage revolvers 38, 39, 40

pepperbox revolvers 36
Perrin revolver 69
Pettengill revolvers 40, 41
Pidault & Cordier revolver 69
Plant revolver 46–47, 47
Pond revolvers 46

Raphael revolver 69
Remington carbines 12, 24, 25, 49

Remington revolvers 35, 36, 36, 46, 57, 57, 67, 70, 70, 71
Remington rifle-muskets 24, 25
Ridgon & Ansley revolvers 43
rifle-muskets 5, 8, 9, 49, 52, 75, 76
Robinson carbine 31, 31
Rogers & Spencer revolvers 41

sabers 4, 5, 7, 51, 66, 70, 71
    import/manufacture 16, 42, 51, 52, 52, 72
    types: M1833 5, 6, 51; M1840 5, 6, 6, 56, 71; M1860 5, 6, 63, 64–65, 71, 71, 72, 76, 76; P1822 6; P1853 51
    use/users 6, 48, 50, 54, 58, 63, 64–65, 66, 71, 72, 73, 75, 76
Savage revolvers 38–39
Sharps carbines 12, 15, 15, 16, 16, 17, 21, 29, 29, 30, 31, 56, 62, 71, 74, 76
Sharps & Hankins carbines 29, 29
Sharps & Hankins derringer 45, 45
Sharps & Hankins rifle 28
shotguns 6, 9, 31, 32, 70, 71, 72
Smith carbine 9, 12, 20–21, 21, 25
Smith & Wesson revolvers 45, 46–47, 46, 73
Spencer carbine 8, 9, 10–11, 12, 13, 17, 51, 55, 57, 62, 63, 64–65, 70, 74, 75, 76, 76
Spencer rifles 8, 12, 13, 51, 62, 63, 64–65, 74
Spiller & Burr revolver 43, 44
Springfield carbines/rifles 5, 75, 75, 76
Springfield pistol carbine 5
Springfield revolvers 46
Springfield rifle-muskets 6–7, 51
Starr carbine 12, 21–22, 22
Starr derringer 45
Starr revolvers 30, 30, 37, 71
swords/swordmakers 42, 44, 51, 52, 72

Tarplay & Garrett carbine 33,
Taylor & Sherrard revolver 43
Terry carbines 33
Tranter revolvers 37, 61, 62
Triplett & Scott carbine/rifles 14, 14
Tucker/Tucker & Sherrard revolvers 43

Union Army cavalry regts (by state): AR 22; CO 14; CT 13, 21; IA 22; IL 14, 21, 22, 27, 39, 69; IN 14, 21; KS 14, 22, 39, 69; KY 14, 17, 27, 39, 69; MA 21; MI 14, 30, 59, 61, 63, 64–65; MO 14, 22, 39, 69; NJ 54, 55; NY 14, 21, 22, 24, 28, 42, 58, 58, 73; OH 14, 21, 24, 26, 39, 27, 41, 71; PA 21, 38, 39, 52, 54, 56, 61, 62; RI 58–59, 59, 71, 73; TN 14; VT 39, 62; WI 28, 39; WV 21, 24, 62, 69
Union Navy, weapons for 7, 8, 12, 25, 26, 29, 37, 39

Volcanic repeating rifle 9, 13
volunteer forces, weapons used 13, 15, 30, 48, 71

Walker revolvers 4, 38
Warner carbines/revolver 12, 28, 46
Webley "Wedge Frame" revolver 62
Wesson carbine 12, 30
Wesson & Leavitts revolver 45–46
Westley Richards shotgun 32
Whitney revolvers 38, 40, 44–45, 71
Winchester repeating rifles 13